MYTH, MEANING, AND ANTIFRAGILE INDIVIDUALISM

ON THE IDEAS OF JORDAN PETERSON

Marc Champagne

SOCIETAS
essays in political
& cultural criticism

imprint-academic.com

Published in the UK by
Imprint Academic Ltd., PO Box 200, Exeter EX5 5YX, UK

Distributed in the USA by
Ingram Book Company,
One Ingram Blvd., La Vergne, TN 37086, USA

ISBN 9781788360142 paperback

A CIP catalogue record for this book is available from the
British Library and US Library of Congress

To Jean-Luc, Louis-Cyr, and Joseph-Arthur,
who are named after mythical heroes
and look like angels when they sleep

Asking people to give up all forms of sacralized belonging and live in a world of purely 'rational' beliefs might be like asking people to give up the Earth and live in colonies orbiting the moon. It can be done, but it would take a great deal of careful engineering, and even after ten generations, the descendants of those colonists might find themselves with inchoate longings for gravity and greenery.

—Jonathan Haidt, *The Righteous Mind: Why Good People Are Divided by Politics and Religion* (2012, p. 307)

[W]e are dividing, and polarizing, and drifting toward chaos. It is necessary, under such conditions, if we are to avoid catastrophe, for each of us to bring forward the truth, as we see it: not the arguments that justify our ideologies, not the machinations that further our ambitions, but the stark pure facts of our existence, revealed to others to see and contemplate, so that we can find common ground and proceed together.

—Jordan B. Peterson, *12 Rules for Life: An Antidote to Chaos* (2018a, p. 361)

Acknowledgements

On the night that I turned in this manuscript, my three year old son told me 'When you die, I will always be there for you'. I want to thank you, Jean-Luc, for letting me experience a love with such a unique metaphysics and grammar. I also want to thank Harri Aaltonen, Dimitri Abbeloos, Micah Amd, Gary Anderson, Hayden Bruce, Adina Cameo, Alex Chapaev, Nathan Robert Cockram, Ron Dart, Vixen Dixon, Derrick Farnham, Mark Frazier, Mark Glouberman, Stephen Hicks, Colin Hutton, David Jopling, François Limoges, Qinruiwen Long, Leslie Marsh, Justice Martens, Tyler Martin, Anil Methipara, Dominique Morisano, Terry Newman, Li Qin, Michal Rusiecki, Shannon Selin, Dania Sheldon, and Håvard Skjekkeland. Naturally, I bear sole responsibility for the views and mistakes in this book.

Contents

Preface

This book will look at how humans use stories to generate meaning, so it seems only fitting to start with a story. I first heard the name 'Jordan Peterson' on March 16, 2017. I can pinpoint this exact date because a prominent lecture was held at the university where I was teaching. After the lecture, a former student asked me what I thought of the lecturer's argument. I had kept mostly silent during the talk, but I confessed that I simply could not believe academics were still peddling vast utopian schemes. This is as old as Plato, so as a professional philosopher I have trained myself in the subtle art of shutting up and smiling politely whenever someone explains their latest 'redistribution' scheme. But after two hours of this, my impatience had risked becoming visible. My student, who shared my impatience, thus tried to cheer me up by telling me about a professor at the University of Toronto who was finally standing up before the crashing wave of social justice hysteria. My response was: that's great, but he won't last. Still, my student was mature and not prone to endorsing just any figure, so his vote of confidence in Peterson left a mark.

A few weeks later, when work slowed down a bit, I Googled Peterson. I eventually came upon a video of him speaking to a class, with his friend Bruce Pardy at his side. Peterson was explaining why no one has a right to not be offended — or something along those lines. I was impressed by what I heard and saw, so I remember telling my partner:

'Hmmm. So far, the UofT prof that my student recommended looks legit…'

When another window of free time opened, I watched a more involved video. I eventually purchased what was at that time his only book, *Maps of Meaning*. The more I studied Peterson's ideas, the more I realized that he was adopting a principled stance. I articulate some criticisms of that stance in the second part of this book. Still, such disagreements aside, here was a thinker who actually *had* a systematic worldview, the lucidity to *explain* it, and the courage to *act* on its basis. These days, such people are in short supply.

Because of this rare combination, Peterson has emerged as a 'public intellectual'—in the strictest and finest sense of that expression. He is public in that he applies his academic training to real-life issues that affect people from all walks of life. He is an intellectual in that he has earned this wide following the hard way, by consistently engaging with real ideas and putting forth real arguments.

The world in which Peterson makes his argumentative interventions is an increasingly confused and confusing one. Indeed, '[p]eople now think nothing of reinventing themselves as a particular set of attributes, however absurd, ideally demonstrating their status as first class victims of a set of social arrangements that have been the reference points for virtually all human societies for tens of thousands of years, which they claim must therefore be overthrown by next Tuesday' (O'Hara 2019, p. 47). In speaking against the foolhardy political implementation of some of these trends, Peterson stands before his detractors with a fortitude reminiscent of Socrates.

Interestingly, Peterson's ideas in psychology help to explain his massive appeal. As he writes: 'The capacity to maintain territorial position when challenged is […] indicative of how "convinced" a given animal is that it can [should] hold its ground […]. This integration constitutes power—*charisma*, in the human realm—made most evident in behavioral display'

(1999, p. 191). The reason why Peterson looks like he believes what he says is that he really believes what he says. In fact, some have suggested that Peterson's *12 Rules for Life* 'are, first and foremost, directed at himself' (Day 2018, p. 13; see, for example, the remarks about not lying in Peterson 2018a, p. 205). This palpable authenticity can be quite attractive. Of course, there is no valid inference from the premise 'A is willing to lose his job for the sake of creed B' to the conclusion 'Creed B must be true/good'. But in ordinary social interactions, we make that leap all the time.

Yet charisma alone cannot explain the remarkable reach that Peterson has attained. To my mind, he stands out from regular pundits because he complements his critical stance with a comprehensive account of what a good life and a good society might look like. At the same time, Peterson has sought to identify what he sees as the source(s) of evil in this world. His tendency is to locate that evil in the individual's lack of responsibility, not in society's alleged oppression. Indeed, Peterson 'has for the past several years been cajoling his fans to stand up instead of stand by' (Shermer 2018, p. 19). This resonates with a lot of people. Every time a new calamity makes the headlines, mainstream commentators and journalists who put ideology before truth lose credibility, while Peterson gains a bigger audience.

In the hands of Peterson, though, such knee-jerk indignation quickly gets converted into something constructive. Peterson thinks there are right and wrong answers to moral questions, but importantly, he does not think those answers can be arrived at by the simplistic power games of group identity politics. As a result, many young people are being exposed—some for the first time—to the option of thinking clearly and taking individual responsibility (instead of emoting loudly and making grand excuses).

One of the things that Peterson's readers and listeners are being exposed to is religion. Peterson is not the only thinker

vying to rehabilitate the place of religion in Western society
(see, for example, Smith 2001), but 'Peterson's Christianity [...]
is a Christianity *revised* for our modern secular age' (Ashford
2020, p. 23; emphasis in original). In his writings and lectures,
Peterson presents an ambitious re-reading of the Bible that
locates this text in humanity's evolutionary history, as it were.
On his telling, the Biblical stories are a collectively authored
attempt to depict the ideal person. The plots and characters that
we find in stories are not devices reserved for aesthetic contemplation. Rather, they play a vital function in guiding the
lives of goal-directed creatures such as ourselves. Christ, we are
told, is a figure who embodies the ideal of 'speaking the truth'
(whatever that means). Questions of exegetical accuracy to the
side, Peterson's twist is to insist that this ideal was reached not
by revelation, but by induction: different folks observed the
conduct of many moral persons, abstracted out the common
denominator in their actions, and then reified the resultant
abstraction in a narrative format. Peterson surmises that the
joint endeavour to construct a 'Logos' or leading principle
predates the Old Testament. The Bible thus offers viable moral
guidance because it distils a large human sample over a long
span of time. Peterson blends the ideas of Jean Piaget and Carl
Jung to elucidate this interplay between personal psychology
and collective archetypes.

Peterson's goal is to unearth reliable interpretative patterns
that range over all conceivable cases, thereby providing a meta-
solution to whatever problem(s) humans might encounter.
Even with free will, nature places serious constraints on what
one can and cannot do (Lawrence and Nohria 2002). The best
strategy for coping with the ignorance and suffering that result
from our finite nature is to take personal responsibility for
one's hardships and constantly negotiate between sticking with
one's beliefs and revising them. This general approach to life,
Peterson argues, was selected for by Darwinian mechanisms
and expressed through cultural channels. Stories are meant to

give us guidance on how to survive a harsh world and achieve balance in our day-to-day lives.

This sweeping account of the human condition has attracted a lot of attention. Every day, magazine articles, videos, blogs, and editorials are released that try to assess Peterson's standing as a thinker (for a survey, see Beverley 2018). Such pieces basically come in two versions. One version says that because Peterson is an original thinker, he should not be dismissed. The other version says that because he is not original, he can be dismissed. To my mind, these two lines of reasoning are misguided, since both are preoccupied with *evaluating* him — when what is called for at this juncture is to *understand* his ideas.

Far from being a liability, I regard this as a straightforward demand of academic professionalism. Understanding an intellectual contribution takes time and effort, so there is a widespread impulse to skip this step. However, the best advice when dealing with any topic, especially a topic deemed controversial, is: take a deep breath, read what is actually written (hearsay without a demonstrable textual basis will not do), and use proven critical-thinking tools. Then, if you want, form an assessment. Note the proper sequence: *scholarship first, judgment after*. At the risk of appearing simplistic, I propose to structure this book after this exact sequence.

Jumping right into criticisms is easy, but how do we even know a topic is spooky if no peer-reviewed books or articles have been published on the subject? Many people have strong opinions about Peterson, but few show any demonstrable command of his written work. A community of scholars cannot reach a justifiable assessment of a stance's merit — negative or positive — if no one ever conducts serious scholarship on that stance. The goal of learning is to evaluate ideas, but such an evaluation will be mere chutzpah if it is not underwritten by a proper understanding (Bloom 1956). At some point, we thinkers have to think.

It may be hyperbolic to claim that Peterson is 'saving Western civilization' (Proser 2020) or that an intellectual movement is afoot (Weiss 2018), but there is definitely significant pushback. Instead of taking the current groundswell of dissent as indicating that certain ideas might be wrong, those in charge take it as indicating that 'another group [...] needs to be educated in the inevitability of diversity or the economic utility of globalisation' (Stacey 2019, p. 1). Filling the demand for different perspectives and honest conversations, platforms such as *Quillette* and *The Rubin Report* have 'skyrocketed in popularity' by discussing 'topics you would find in a typical Peterson lecture' (Lovins 2018, pp. 7–8). In mainstream venues, however, few engage with what Peterson actually says or writes. What we find instead is a concerted effort to push Peterson outside the Overton window of acceptability by whatever means necessary (innuendo, guilt by association, smears, etc.).

Vigorous disagreements are fine, but I don't like bullies, wherever they are found (Shapiro 2013). So while my study of Peterson began as a hobby, it gradually climbed up my ladder of academic priority, culminating in this book.

Peterson has nevertheless made it hard for professional academics to engage with his ideas. Some obstacles are format related. Peterson presents many of his ideas extemporaneously in online videos, but this makes those ideas hard to cite and trace reliably. I've also had to consider secondary sources from non-academic venues that I would ordinarily not turn to (newspapers, self-published books, etc.). However, some obstacles are more substantial. Peterson often describes his contribution as a scientific one, but I think this self-description obscures more than it reveals, since it conflates two kinds of intellectual projects. On the one hand, Peterson has been publishing a steady stream of peer-reviewed articles in psychology journals. These articles, most of which are co-authored, typically present quantitative analyses of narrow, technical

CBT as Peterson's real experts

topics. His most cited paper as a first co-author, for example, is about the effects of alcohol intoxication on cognitive functions (Peterson *et al.* 1990). It is doubtful that those drawn to Peterson's ideas regard this empirical study as a life-changing masterpiece. On the other hand, when Peterson published *Maps of Meaning* in 1999, he essentially presented a Theory of Everything. While Peterson is a respectable academic, his credentials (and citation count) were achieved mainly in narrow co-authored psychology papers.

Now, in Peterson's defence, one could argue that his 'detailing and promotion of hero mythology can be thought of as the original, romanticized, and richer version of the colder, clinical application of exposure-based treatments that are derived from cognitive-behavioral therapy (CBT) — one of the most evidence-based psychological treatments that we have for a myriad of presenting problems, including depressive, anxiety, and addictive disorders' (Stea 2018, p. 25; see Butler *et al.* 2006). Still, in the relevant fields, such as philosophy, Peterson is basically self-taught.

His allusions to science thus invite serious criticism. As many critics have pointed out, Peterson has a tendency to repackage pearls of wisdom that already enjoy wide circulation in popular culture. His critics (e.g. Robinson 2018) are thus dismayed to find an author receiving so much attention and praise for enjoining us to tell the truth (Peterson 2018a, pp. 203–30) and pursue what is meaningful (2018a, pp. 161–201). In the eyes of many, expounding such well-worn platitudes does not constitute a ground-breaking achievement.

Is Jordan Peterson an original thinker? Our first reflex upon hearing this question should be to ask: original by what standard? By taking on the language of science, Peterson has taken on the standards of science. Judged by those standards, there is some truth to the charge that many of his ideas fail to demonstrate much originality. Yet to my mind, the proper response is not to exclaim 'Gotcha!' and conveniently ignore what Peterson has to say. Instead, the proper response is to call into question Peterson's own way of describing what he does. Peterson may insist that he is putting forward scientific work, but authors are not always the persons best placed to categorize the genre under which their writings fall.

The moment we let go of the label 'science', we lift the over-bearing expectation of novelty that comes with that activity. For instance, if Peterson claims that 'ideas x, y, and z have implicitly guided human actions for as long as humans have existed', is it really a reproach to say that x, y, and z are things we already know? Peterson's account *predicts* that the deep-seated myths and moral insights that he discusses will, when rendered explicit, seem familiar to us. It cannot be a criticism of his account, then, to point out that this prediction bears out. What Peterson says indeed sounds familiar, but if we understand Peterson's main claim, we see that this is not a flaw—it's the point.

Originality is nice when it can be had. However, there are other attributes one can look for in ideas, including clarification, edification, systematization, and even inspiration. The age-old myths and archetypes that inform our conceptions and guide our actions are thus definitely worth discussing, despite our prior familiarity with them. In fact, one could argue that they merit careful study precisely because they are closely wedded to our lives. Sometimes, we must learn something new that we do not know. Other times, though, we must learn anew something that we already know. If we uncritically demand novelty and change from all theories, we risk blinding ourselves to this genuine intellectual possibility, which I see Peterson's work as exploring.

Peterson agrees with Friedrich Nietzsche that our civilized culture is an outgrowth of our animal nature. As a result, the foundations for knowledge and ethics posited by the best philosophies are 'in fact, far less a discovery than a recognition, a remembering, a return and a homecoming to a remote, primordial, and inclusive household of the soul, out of which those concepts grew originally' (Nietzsche 1966, p. 27; quoted in Peterson 1999, p. 79). Peterson argues that, owing to their evolutionary pedigree, many established social practices and institutions deserve to be maintained. Now, one may take issue with the specific practices and institutions that Peterson singles out as worth keeping. However, one cannot define inquiry in a way that automatically blames Peterson for failing to be reformist (or reformist enough). He is not trying to be.

Deplorably, the label 'conservative' is something one gets 'accused' of these days. Indeed, what Roger Scruton said about academia in the 1960s arguably applies today:

> To be a conservative, I was told, was to be on the side of age against youth, the past against the future, authority against innovation, the 'structures' against spontaneity and life. It was enough to understand this to recognize that one had no choice, as a free-thinking intellectual, save to reject conservatism. The choice remaining was […] [d]o we improve society bit by bit, or do we rub it out and start again? On the whole my contemporaries favoured the second option […].
> (Scruton 2009, p. 3)

For reasons that I will explain in the final chapter, I find the label 'conservative' (and that of 'liberal') to be confused and unhelpful. Still, it can have a sensible definition, provided we keep in mind that '[a]s an epistemic stance, all that *political* conservatism claims is that we do not have a predictive science of politics on grounds of *complexity*; and that it is epistemically prudential, for a whole tissue of reasons, to preserve the existing, albeit flawed, advantages, rather than to instigate a wholesale trading in of inherited practices for the completely unknown' (Marsh 2018, pp. 167–68). Formulated this way, conservatism cannot be laughed out of court. At the very least, if one is going to hold Peterson accountable to standards that

'Conservative' vs 'liberal'

privilege novelty and change, one must provide non-circular arguments for why those standards are relevant, applicable, or worthwhile.

All too often, critics simply take it for granted that demonstrating originality is of paramount importance. Scientists are expected to make original contributions, so it certainly doesn't help that Peterson aligns himself with scientists. I submit, though, that this entire way of approaching his work is unhelpful. He is scientifically informed, yes; but the core claims that have won him a wide following are philosophical, not scientific.

A philosophy is a set of explicit or implicit views about what there is (metaphysics), how one knows this (epistemology), and what one should do, both as a person (ethics) and as a society (politics). Everyone has a philosophy; the only choice is whether one adopts it critically or uncritically. Our parents or guardians and surrounding culture determine our first philosophical commitments (for better or worse), so to read with an open mind is to shop for better and better replacement parts. At the moment, those wishing to acquaint themselves with Peterson's philosophy in a written format can turn only to his two books, *12 Rules for Life: An Antidote to Chaos* (2018) and *Maps of Meaning: The Architecture of Belief* (1999). *12 Rules* is meant to be accessible, but the book's size and many digressions make it a poor spokesperson for the claim that Peterson's thinking is systematic. As for *Maps of Meaning*, one must already be convinced that Peterson is worth reading before committing oneself to such a hefty and opaque text. These obstacles may explain why 'many of his most ardent supporters have not read much, if any, of his published material' (Day 2018, p. 5). There is a pressing need, then, for a clear and concise commentary on Peterson's ideas. Sometimes, the best way to learn about someone's ideas is by reading someone *else* discussing those ideas (getting a fresh perspective doesn't hurt, either).

Taken together, Peterson's academic neglect and wide following are 'proof of how completely at odds institutions of higher education have become with their essential purpose, and from the young people who seek the education they are meant to provide' (Blackwood 2019). Trying to rectify this, my discussion will circle around the themes of myth, meaning, and antifragile individualism, which figure prominently in Peterson's books and lectures. I am not concerned with Jordan Peterson's persona or the gossip surrounding him. I am concerned with his *ideas*.

I do not aim to change anyone's mind about anything. My hope instead is that this book can serve as a launch pad for further academic engagement with Peterson's work. Still, writing about Peterson's ideas is mission impossible. No author —Peterson included—can possibly master all the disciplines that he touches upon. So, judged by the standards of the specialist, any work covering Peterson's ideas is bound to have flaws, omissions, and shortcomings. Since fallibility is part and parcel of the human condition, I do not think one should wait for perfection before discussing ideas and arguments. In academia as in real life, we have to start somewhere. Also like real life, the hard part is to start.

There is nevertheless a risk of being mistaken and/or misunderstood, especially when the topic is so new and evolving so rapidly. Indeed, a mere three years will have elapsed between my first encounter with Peterson's name and the release of this book. I could have stretched the slingshot longer —or picked a safer topic, for that matter. But '[b]itter divides are poisoning our politics' and '[o]pportunities for course-correction are dwindling' (Murray 2019). To miss out on the issues that Peterson addresses would be to miss one of the great debates of our age.

Part 1

Exposition

Chapter 1

Coping with our own ignorance

Consider the following true statement: we are conceived, we live, and then we die. This truth ranges over every human, past, present, and future. Yet such broad statements are rare, because the more we graft words onto a statement, the more we generate exceptions that shrink its range. Does this mean that someone looking for sweeping truths about life's meaning must make do only with platitudes? Peterson has set himself the task of making general but true claims about what happens —and what ought to happen—between the bookends of conception and death.

At first glance, one might think that such a project is too grand to be feasible. After all, given the incredible diversity of lives and backgrounds, what sorts of descriptions and prescriptions could possibly apply to all persons? A more modest outlook seems to be in order. Academics certainly privilege narrow studies. Even in lay milieus, it is common to write books about more mundane problems—losing weight, finding the right partner, building a successful business, raising better children, etc. On the surface, Peterson's *12 Rules for Life* looks modelled after such books. Peterson's goal, however, is more abstract. As he puts it, the real problem is the fact that we have problems. So in his quest to find general truths, Peterson begins with the following certainty, which we can add to the shortlist of conception, life, and death: we do not know everything. As Peterson explains in a keystone passage:

> The infinite human capacity for error means that encounter with the unknown is inevitable. [...] The (variable) existence of the unknown, paradoxically enough, *can therefore be regarded as an environmental constant.* Adaptation to the 'existence' of this domain must occur, therefore, in every culture, and in every historical period—regardless of the particulars of any given social or biological circumstance. (Peterson 1999, p. 47)

We do not know anything about some random human who lived 3,000 years ago, but we can affirm with confidence that this human did not know everything. As embodied creatures, we must act in the world, so we have no choice but to (implicitly or explicitly) make maps of the natural and social environments that surround us. Invariably, though, there will be times when those maps fail, on a small or a large scale. Peterson thus wants to articulate a general theory of how we cope when these systems of beliefs break down.

In a way, Peterson's training as a clinician colours his philosophical approach, since he wants to diagnose personal and social ailments in the hope of making people's lives better. Interestingly, he thinks that to achieve this goal one must first step back and see the big picture. Professional scholars are usually interested in narrow, technical questions. So if analysis is zooming in to divide an issue into smaller parts, then synthesis is zooming out to unite various issues into an integrated whole. Peterson thus 'aims to draw his conclusions based on a scientific principle called consilience of findings [...]. This means that Peterson aims to link facts and principles across disciplines of study to help ground his claims in evidence' (Stea 2018, p. 25; see Wilson 1999).

Such a synthetic style of thinking may have fallen out of fashion, but it was central to thinkers such as Aristotle and Epicurus who, in addition to investigating nature and human nature, mobilized their findings in the service of an even more important question: what would constitute a meaningful life?

Peterson sometimes writes poetically about meaning (see, for example, Peterson 2018a, p. 201), but I want to focus on his more tangible theorizing. In keeping with the search for truly general patterns, Peterson proposes that 'meaning' has a three-part structure. The first part is *what is* (see Peterson 1999, p. 14). Peterson's account thus begins where all accounts must begin, namely, where one happens to find oneself. As Heidegger (1996) said, we are each 'thrown' into the world (for Peterson's appreciation of Heidegger, see Peterson 2018a, p. xxxi, as well as Peterson and Flanders 2002, pp. 436–37). Like it or not, one already occupies a distinct spot on the planet, one already has parents or guardians, one already knows (at least) one language, one already has taken on a host of habits (good and bad), one already has a host of personality traits (again, good and bad), and so on. We have no choice about any of this. So even if one is not happy with one's current situation, the very act of '[g]etting to point "b" presupposes that you are at point "a" —you can't plan movement in the absence of an initial position' (Peterson 1999, p. 22).

We may not be able to alter where we are and what we have done, but we can certainly choose what we will do next. Yet no amount of information will amount to a decision. As Peterson is fond of saying, looking harder at an open field will not tell you where to walk in that field (or whether one should step on that field at all). A choice must therefore be made. If I want to be in the eastern portion of the field, I must walk in an easterly direction. Likewise, when I walk in an easterly direction, I implicitly endorse the east as my aim. This is the second part of Peterson's basic model: we must decide *what should be*. To act is to privilege one action over other possible actions, including the action of staying still. Hence, '[t]he fact that point "b" constitutes the end goal means that it is valenced more highly than point "a" — that it is a place more desirable, when considered against the necessary contrast of the current position' (Peterson 1999, pp. 22–23).

The freedom to pick this end-goal gives us some leeway, but it also gives us a distinctive responsibility, in so far as we must now figure out *how we should act*. This is the third component of Peterson's three-part model. When we step onto an open field, we are not pushed by some gust of wind behind our back. Rather, we are pulled toward a goal. So between the starting point of 'a' and the destination 'b', there is the journey 'c', which will transport us (literally or figuratively) from the former to the latter. 'We conceive of a path connecting present to future. This path is "composed" of the behaviors required to produce the transformations we desire' (Peterson 1999, p. 29).

As this brief sketch shows, Peterson's account of meaning is goal-directed through and through. Living creatures are all striving to realize an inchoate or articulate vision of what should be. Thus, '[o]ur most fundamental maps of meaning [...] portray *the motivational value of our current state*, conceived of *in contrast to a hypothetical ideal*, accompanied *by plans of action*, which are our pragmatic notions about how to get what we want' (1999, p. 22). This is the model onto which Peterson will graft the rest of his ideas.

The only chunk of matter under one's control is one's body. As a result of this limited range, the goal of becoming, say, an architect is too abstract to be put into practice. So, concretely speaking, all that one can do at a given time is study a particular book chapter, tap a particular computer key, and so on. However, when one strings together such discrete actions in a deliberate way, one moves in the direction that one imagines and seeks. We all pursue the goal of living, and this pursuit compels us to pursue a host of sub-goals, such as eating, sleeping, working — which are in turn comprised of sub-goals.

A sub-goal 'would therefore have the same motivational significance as the goal, although at lesser intensity (as it is only one small part of a large and more important whole)' (Peterson 1999, p. 27). To *be* an architect is to *do* what architects do. If the big goal matters, then every action that leads to that goal, no matter how little, partakes in its significance. Peterson thus contends that our lives feel most meaningful when we aim for a challenging goal and work daily to achieve it.

Peterson does not claim that achieving one's goal(s) is easy, but neither does he claim that achieving one's goal(s) is impossible. So '[w]here Freud made great contributions in explaining neuroses by, among other things, focusing on understanding what we might call a failed-hero story (that of Oedipus), Jordan [Peterson] focuse[s] on triumphant heroes' (Doidge 2018, p. xvii). A tenable account of human experience should not just focus on psychological pathologies and theorize what happens when things go wrong; it should also define mental health and theorize what happens when things go right.

When we pursue a goal, we necessarily do so without any evidence that the goal in question will be achieved. Hence, '[t]he goal is an imaginary state [...] that only exists in fantasy, as something (potentially) preferable to the present' (Peterson 1999, p. 13). Craving for some ironclad proof of success in one's projects would thus be misplaced. The only way to know for certain that one has the ability to become an architect would be to have constructed buildings to one's credit. By that point, one's accomplishments would attest to one's abilities in an undeniable manner. However, this very fact would propel one's professional standing to the starting point of *what is*, since the goal of being an architect would already be a done deal (in the same way that when 'tomorrow' finally comes, it transforms into 'today'). By the same token, the end-state of *what should be* would be nudged away, forcing one to choose a goal all over again. Enduring habits and social ties may make it easier for one to continue being an architect, but, since humans are not dominoes, nothing in a given decision mandates that there be a series of future decisions resembling it. Hence, if we stay on a path, it is because we choose to stay on that path (compare this to Beauvoir 2004, pp. 89–141, as well as Champagne and Gladstein 2015).

For humans, the three-part structure of 'what is + what should be = how one should act' is held together by *story*. Our lives are lived not as a sequence of events, but as an ongoing drama, with characters, a back-story, cliff-hangers, plot twists, foreshadowing, denouements, etc. Hence, our behaviours are not only goal-directed but also narratively-structured.

Interestingly, there is evidence that if one engages in some kind of conscious self-authoring, one is more likely to stay on track and achieve one's goals (Morisano *et al.* 2010; Schippers *et al.* 2015). People trying to improve their lives and minimize their (inevitable) hardships do not have to draw their plans from scratch. On the contrary, Peterson contends that we 'presently possess in accessible and complete form the traditional wisdom of a large part of the human race — possess accurate description [*sic*] of the myths and rituals that contain and condition the implicit and explicit values of almost everyone who has ever lived' (1999, p. 12). If one tires of reading psychological theories about what happens when things go wrong, one can turn to these historical sources for a sketch of what happens when things go right.

The humanities have no trouble discussing narratives, but natural science is not quite sure what to make of them. Yet Peterson believes that, in principle, narratives can and should be integrated into a biological account (for the neuroscience of narratives, see Mar 2004). The stories we tell are encoded practices that have been selected over time by evolution to serve purely biological ends. A story will be remembered when it fosters human flourishing and forgotten when it hinders (or has no bearing on) that flourishing. Peterson's methodological assumption, then, is that the relative age of a story attests to its evolutionary pedigree. This assumption permits a key inference, namely that the further back in time we find a given narrative structure, the more safely we can assume that it served human ends. This inference is not 100% certain, but it lends old beliefs a measure of credence. According to Peterson, even recent fictional works are beholden to this general rule. Some Disney movies, for example, enjoy a wide viewership because they tap into narrative structures (hero versus villain, overbearing mother, prodigal son, etc.) that have been told and retold for ages (Peterson 2018a, pp. 324–26).

The archetypes of Carl Jung help Peterson classify the various narrative patterns that govern our fundamental understanding of ourselves and the world (Jung 2014; Segal 1999, pp. 67–97; Stein 1998). Invoking the Jungian notion of archetype to elucidate mythical ideas can seem like compounding obscurity with more obscurity. Indeed, Peterson attempts to give 'functional definitions of concepts that, for many, seem empty at best and a naïve, wish fulfillment desires [sic] at worst' (Lovins 2018, p. 86). Yet Peterson's use of the notion of archetype is different from Jung's, since he ascribes to some narratives an evolutionary lineage going back to non-human ancestors (Peterson 2018a, pp. 1–28).

Despite the diversity of lives and life forms, the root situation that stories are constrained by is fairly straightforward. The starting point is the brute fact that '[h]umans inhabit a world that has limits. […] Vulnerabilities, then, are a precondition for the wonderful and remarkable possibility of being human' (Steem and Steem 2020, p. 189). To be alive is to face challenges, experience suffering, and struggle to overcome the two. The most enduring stories are those that describe this shared predicament and guide us in our struggle.

Building on his three-part model of meaning, Peterson claims that 'current state, ideal future state, and means of active mediation—constitute the necessary and sufficient preconditions for the weaving of the most simple narrative' (1999, p.

22). This allows Peterson to classify myths into four basic categories, depending on which part they emphasize (Peterson 1999, p. 16):

(1) Myths that describe a current stable state, good or bad.
(2) Myths that describe the surprising appearance of something that threatens the state of (1).
(3) Myths that describe the dissolution of (1) into chaos as a consequence of (2).
(4) Myths that describe how the stability of (1) is regained, despite the challenges posed by (2) and (3).

Narratives will vary depending on whether they foreground established customs or the need to update those customs (in light of their tangible failings). There are stories that confirm what we already know and stories that seek to teach us something new. Peterson (1999, p. 29) explicitly compares his account with Thomas Kuhn's distinction between 'normal' and 'revolutionary' science (Kuhn 1996, pp. 10, 92). Normal narratives are more like cooking recipes that tell us how to cook a dish we already know and desire. By contrast, revolutionary narratives introduce entirely new dishes to us. Given the richness and diversity of human experiences, both types of narratives have a role to play. There is a time and a place for conserving established social and habitual structures, just as there is a time and place for reforming them in light of new information.

Peterson writes that '[t]he hero is [sic] narrative representation of the individual eternally willing to take creative action' (1999, p. 186). Interestingly though, the person recounting the exploits of a hero cannot be too heroic. As Gottschall reminds us, when stories depended on storytellers instead of books for their continued existence, '[t]ribal storytellers who undercut time-honored values—who insulted group norms—faced severe consequences' (2013, p. 133). Not only can an offensive book be burned but so can an offensive speaker. Challenging ingrained beliefs thus contains an element of risk.

In keeping with Peterson's synthetic philosophical approach, the general distinctions that he puts forward are meant to range over all major world cultures and religions. Naturally, backing this up with evidence would require a great deal of comparative work. However, like all humans, Peterson starts where he finds himself. He thus uses mainly the Christian tradition to illustrate his four-fold classification of myths:

> The traditional Christian (and not just Christian) notion that man has fallen from an original 'state of grace' into his current morally degenerate and emotionally unbearable condition—accompanied by a desire for the 'return to Paradise'—constitutes a single example of this 'metamyth'. Christian morality can therefore be reasonably regarded as the 'plan of action' whose aim is re-establishment, or establishment, or attainment (sometimes in the 'hereafter') of the 'kingdom of God', the ideal future. (Peterson 1999, p. 17)

Because taking stock of where and who we *are* does not tell us where and who we *should* be, we need a vision that will move us forward. This vision will naturally vary from culture to culture. But given that all humans tell stories and struggle to find meaning in their lives, it should, in principle, be possible to give a general account of storytelling and struggling. Peterson therefore surmises that '[c]areful comparative analysis of this great body of religious philosophy might allow us to provisionally determine the nature of essential human motivation and morality' (1999, p. 12).

Chapter 2

The territory of the known, the territory of the unknown

No matter how adept we become at mapping the world around us, our inherent limitations ensure that this map will have gaps and inaccuracies. Importantly, these gaps and inaccuracies cannot be detected by introspection. On the contrary, we realize that we were wrong only when we confront events that we could not foresee. Peterson thus suggests that, ultimately, all experiences can be sorted into two fundamental categories: chaos and order. 'Chaos' is what happens when our habits fail us and our undertakings unexpectedly collapse. 'Order', by contrast, is what happens when our habits serve us well and everything is going according to plan.

Evolutionary forces may shape biological attributes in powerful and wondrous ways, but no mutation could ever equip an organism with the power to forecast future events with absolute accuracy. The best nature can do is equip organisms with a capacity for attention. When something unexpected happens, we can at least focus on 'that' event, even if we have no clue 'what' is happening. Thus, '[w]e attend, involuntarily, to those things that occur contrary to our predictions — that occur in spite of our desires, as expressed in expectation. That involuntary attention comprises a large part of what we refer to when we say "consciousness"' (Peterson 1999, p. 21; see Clark 2013). Being in a state of order produces emotions such as calm (and, at the pathological extreme, boredom), whereas being in a state of chaos produces emotions such as fear, excitement, and anger.

These moments of chaos and order happen at different scales. A small-scale encounter with chaos, for example, could be stepping onto an elevator that usually functions, only to find out that it now does not. One clearly intended to go somewhere by taking the elevator (i.e. the envisioned end-state of what should be, discussed in Peterson's three-part model). This aim gave rise to a more or less articulate plan of action (i.e. the connecting state of what we should do) — in this case, taking an elevator. However, this small-scale plan collapsed when it encountered something genuinely unexpected, namely, the broken elevator. When I find that the elevator is broken, '[t]he map I was using to evaluate my environment has been invalidated' (1999, p. 46). At that moment, I experience chaos.

We routinely experience chaos, so most of us are adept at making minor adjustments to return to order. It is not very complicated, for instance, to take another elevator, or to reach one's destination by using a staircase or other route. We are like the ship's captain who, despite heading in a specific direction (in the longer term), constantly turns the boat's steering wheel left or right (in the shorter term) to accommodate for wind and waves.

> When we are in the domain of the known, so to speak, there is no reason for fear. Outside that domain, panic reigns. It is for this reason that we dislike having our plans disrupted, and cling to what we understand. This conservative strategy does not always work, however, because what we understand about the present is not always necessarily sufficient to deal with the future. This means that we have to be able to modify what we understand, even though to

do so is to risk our own undoing. The trick, of course, is to modify and yet to remain secure. This is not so simple. (Peterson 1999, p. 18)

Peterson recognizes that most 'individuals will go to almost any length to ensure that their protective cultural "stories" remain intact' (1999, p. 18). Sometimes, though, our habitual ways of living fail on a grand scale, despite our best efforts. This is the case, for instance, when a person living a peaceful domestic life suddenly learns that their lifelong partner has been unfaithful. Episodes like these expose us to chaos in a more profound way than mundane experiences, like broken elevators. Yet despite the change in affective intensity, the way back to order is the same, in so far as we must respond by devising new plans of action.

Peterson does not have a one-size-fits-all solution to all human ills—one-on-one consultation would be needed to actually know about specific problems and prescribe specific remedies. He does, however, encourage us to accept that no matter how orderly our lives may feel at any given point, chaos will eventually remind us of our frailty. This is most apparent in the fact that, ultimately, we will all fail to stay alive.

Although the breakdown of our aims is guaranteed by death, chaos is not always a bad thing. Friedrich Nietzsche, from whom Peterson draws much inspiration, famously said, 'What doesn't kill me makes me stronger' (2005, p. 157). This is the bumper sticker for a trait that is best called *antifragility*. Antifragility is not just resilience. Whereas '[t]he resilient resists shocks and stays the same; the antifragile gets better' (Taleb 2014, p. 3; for a discussion of Peterson and antifragility, see Markey-Towler 2018).

'Getting better' would seem to be a synonym for 'learning'. Sadly, many professors and students in universities in Canada, the United States, and parts of Europe have accepted the idea that individuals have a right to never experience discomfort (including the discomfort of feeling offended). The deleterious effects of this idea on 'young people, universities, and, more generally, liberal democracies' have been ably discussed by Lukianoff and Haidt (2018, p. 4). What Peterson adds is a broader worldview in which to embed the idea that 'as hard and as frustrating as it may be, the benefits from exploring our competing ideas can make that cost worthwhile, if we can get the ground rules of a constructive and civil debate in place' (Penk 2019). The most important lesson to learn from learning is that dragging something from the territory of the unknown to the territory of the known is often scary, but it is always beneficial.

Such a culture of open inquiry is not a given but a tradition, that is, a set of guidelines and personality traits that have to be replicated from generation to generation. If Peterson is right, this replication takes place in a narrative medium. Nassim Nicholas Taleb—arguably the chief describer of antifragility—concedes that '[m]etaphors and stories are far more potent (alas) than ideas' (2007, p. xxvii). It is not that professors in all subject matters should devote some classes to discussing world literature. Rather, professors should seek to embody heroic features in their very classroom practice. Every lecture is an unfolding story (Peterson 2018a, p. 251), so the person in charge of telling that story should display, in his or her micro-choices, the various traits that make one better equipped to cope with ignorance and confront life's adversity. How is antifragility conducive to the pursuit of knowledge? The most powerful way to answer that question is to demonstrate it in practice—and let role-modelling take care of the rest. With that in mind, Peterson 'serves as a role model for many, teaching them that facts do matter. […] For Peterson, growth comes from constantly questioning himself, and being open to seeing another person's point of view, even where the disagreements are profound' (Higgins 2018).

Yet, however practical antifragility may be in the long run, it is natural for an organism to prefer the path of least resistance. Peterson's story about stories thus makes provisions for the fact that unless we are given tangible cause to re-examine what we know and do, we rarely take the initiative to increase or improve what we already know and do. A real hero does not engage in bravado. Voluntary exposure to some measure of adversity and unpredictability can nevertheless be beneficial. Consider technology. Each technological advance was, at some point, a confrontation with the unknown or chaos, in Peterson's sense. Yet, over time, we often come to see the benefits of a novel device. Even when a given piece of equip-ment is well known, there are always possibilities in its use that elude us. This is applicable at all levels. Meeting new persons, for example, is clearly an encounter with chaos, since we cannot (yet) predict how this person will act. Even so, meeting new people is among the most enriching experiences a human can have. When we have mapped out how a person acts and reacts, there are always possibilities that elude us. The same could be said of visiting new places, trying new foods, and playing new sports. A meaningful life needs chaos, since only chaos can bring novel contents into our stream of consciousness.

Peterson applies these fundamental categories of chaos and order to different domains, which he represents as territories in concentric rings (see 1999, p. 136). The innermost territory is personal. This is where we are most at home (even if the con-tents of one's inner home can sometimes be in severe disarray). Next in terms of familiarity and security are social structures. Here, we find ourselves surrounded by customs, institutions, and norms that regulate our relationships. Outside the social sphere, we find the vast territory of nature. Peterson's sub-divisions are meant to stress that regardless of whether a domain is personal, social, or natural, we can profitably understand that domain as involving moments of chaos and moments of order.

Ideologies, on this view, are oversimplified stories that portray only partial aspects of reality. Everybody has some good and some bad within them, but an ideology will neglect one side. All societies have beneficial and harmful aspects, but an ideology will neglect one side. Nature, too, is not all good or all bad, but an ideology will overlook one side. For instance, many environmentalist narratives depict nature as all good but people and societies as all bad (Peterson 2018a, pp. 13–14; see, for example, DeLuca 2007). This picture quickly organizes a host of facts, actions, and events. Using it, we know who to blame whenever things go wrong. However, an ideology cannot yield worthwhile practical results, because it fails to fully map the world. The advantages associated with gaining civilized control over a wild piece of land will, for instance, be invisible to an environmentalist ideologue. Peterson's account therefore gives us tools to understand how such ideological possession operates.

> Ideologies are attractive, not least to the educated modern mind […]. Their power stems from their incomplete but effective appropriation of mythological ideas. Their danger stems from their attractiveness, in combination with their incompleteness. Ideologies tell only part of the story, but tell that part as if it were complete. This means that they do not take into account vast domains of the world. It is incautious to act in the world as if only a set of its constituent elements exist. The ignored elements conspire, so to speak, as a consequence of their repression, and make their existence known, inevitably, in some undesirable manner. Knowledge of the grammar of mythology might well constitute an antidote to ideological gullibility. (Peterson 1999, p. 217)

Our brains, personalities, and social institutions have all evolved to negotiate the never-ending balancing act between habit and innovation. 'Too much modification brings chaos. Too little modification brings stagnation' (Peterson 1999, p. 18). Although Peterson sometimes uses psychology and neuro-science to express this elemental cartography of experience, he is adamant that a map along these lines has been at work for millennia, in our most persistent myths and legends. Instructions for how to achieve balance are encrypted into familiar stories, which can be mined for their hidden wisdom.

> Genuine myths are capable of representing the totality of conflicting forces, operating in any given situation. Every positive force has its omnipresent and eternal 'enemy'. The beneficial aspect of the 'natural environment' is therefore properly viewed in light of its capacity to arbitrarily inflict suffering and death. The protective and sheltering capacity of society is therefore understood in light of its potent tendency to tyranny and the elimination of necessary diversity. The heroic aspect of the individual is regarded in light of the ever-lurking figure of the adversary: arrogant, cowardly and cruel. A story accounting for all of these 'constituent elements of reality' is balanced and stable, in contrast to an ideology—and far less likely to produce an outburst of social psychopathology. (Peterson 1999, pp. 217–18)

Standard hero mythology, for instance, recounts the story of a person who leaves their comfort zone, faces the unknown, restores order, and returns to share this accomplishment with the rest of the community. One of the morals conveyed by this narrative pattern is that we all benefit from heroic triumphs. For instance, few of us could have arrived at the great discoveries and cures of prominent scientists. Even so, we are all better for their efforts. Just as we now honour these heroic figures in textbooks and encyclopaedias, able prehistoric hunters would have been honoured by their tribe or village with cave paintings and songs.

Peterson believes that a pattern can be discerned in these seemingly disparate examples. Some stable personal, social, or natural order was threatened by an encroaching unknown, which has now been rendered known thanks to the bravery of an antifragile individual. Humans acted out their fledgling grasp of these patterns in dreams and rituals, long before they articulated them verbally. Likewise, Peterson (2018a, pp. xxxii-iii) confesses that he first had to dream of this idea before meticulously articulating it in *Maps of Meaning*.

Peterson thus uses a notion from the humanities — myth — to connect domains of inquiry usually studied by natural and social scientists. He is less interested in discovering a local piece of knowledge than he is in formulating a comprehensive framework in which all knowledge claims and theories can find a proper place. Even the vast expanse of the unknown is given a place in Peterson's cartography. This unknown could be either beneficial or harmful. 'The *worst* the unknown could be, in general, is death (or, perhaps, lengthy suffering followed by death)', whereas '[t]he *best* the unknown could be [...] [is] to be wealthy (or at least free from want), possessed of good health, wise and well-loved' (Peterson 1999, p. 26). For instance, it is currently unclear whether advances in biotechnology and artificial intelligence will free or enslave humankind. If we had clarity on this, we would know whether to approach or with-draw. We can respond, if we wish, but right now we cannot formulate an informed response. Vacillating between approach and withdrawal is taxing and unpleasant, because we 'cannot move forwards and backwards, cannot stop and go, simulta-neously' (Peterson 1999, p. 41). Even so, we have to resist the urge to project our hopes and fears onto this uncharted terri-tory of our map.

Peterson remarks that '[w]e tend to view the "environment" as something "objective", but one of its most basic features—familiarity, or lack thereof—is something virtually defined by the subjective' (1999, p. 48). Peterson's point is not that the world is pliable or that anything goes. His point is that the comfort we find in our environment is actually an accomplishment. The tricky part is that this accomplishment tends to efface itself. Indeed, the whole value of declaring a space safe is to turn off our exploratory systems. Philosophical reflection nevertheless allows us to see that the many things we take for granted—that the chair we sit on will not break, for instance—are moments of order superimposed on a default mixture of order and chaos. One virtue of this Petersonian account is that when chaos creeps back in and the chair *does* break, this anomalous event will not look overly mysterious, since an element of mystery was countenanced from the start. We simply lose sight of this when things go well.

Disorder is thus defined and identified by contrasting it with order. Peterson discusses a fairly straightforward experiment where a subject is exposed to 'a repetitious sequence of otherwise predictable tones' through stereo headphones (1999, p. 50). When experimenters 'randomly and rarely insert a tone that differs in frequency', this 'odd-ball event' will 'evoke a pattern of cortical electrical activity that differs from that produced by the predictable tones' (1999, p. 50). The brain goes into cost-effective mode as soon as it can, but it suddenly jumps back into action when a predictable habit gets ruptured. 'When something occurs that is not intended—when the actual outcome, as interpreted, does not match the desired outcome, as posited—the hippocampus shifts mode and prepares to update cortical memory storage' (1999, p. 54).

Recall that, for Peterson, the unknown is 'the matrix from which all conditional knowledge emerges' (1999, p. 48). To the extent that organisms have adapted to such a world, Peterson's metaphysics entails an epistemology where knowers must be suited to recognize the contrast between chaos and order. As a result, '[t]he constant and universal presence of the incomprehensible in the world has elicited adaptive response [*sic*] from us and from all other creatures with highly developed nervous systems. We have evolved to operate successfully in a world eternally composed of the predictable, in paradoxical juxtaposition with the unpredictable' (1999, p. 52). Our involuntary detection of the 'odd-ball' tone in a sequence is a concrete example of this. We do not always encounter the unusual, but we are always on the lookout for the unusual.

To count as anomalous, an experience merely has to deviate from an established pattern. This deviation is enough for an organism to suspect that it may be in the presence of a threat. By default, everything we experience is suspect—the burden is on subsequent experience to show otherwise. One consequence of Peterson's stance is that '[t]hings are not irrelevant'; rather, '[t]hey are *rendered* irrelevant, as a consequence of (successful) exploratory behavior' (1999, p. 55). Hence, at the most fundamental level,

> human beings do not learn to fear new objects or situations, or even really 'learn' to fear something that previously appeared safe, when it manifests a dangerous property. Fear is the *a priori* position, the natural response to everything for which no structure of behavioral adaptation has been designed and inculcated. Fear is the *innate* reaction to everything that has not been rendered predictable [...]. Classical behavioral psychology is wrong in the same manner our folk presumptions are wrong: fear is not secondary, not learned; security is secondary, learned. (Peterson 1999, pp. 56–57)

Peterson observes that in standard behavioural conditioning experiments involving trained rats, the 'rat was inevitably afraid as soon as he was placed in the new experimental environment' (1999, p. 58). The animal thus responds to the anomalous displacement with fear *before* any experimental protocol is implemented. When a rat is plunged into an unfamiliar territory, whatever map it had relied on until that point necessarily falls short. Revising this map takes some time. So until chaos is dispelled and order is restored, the animal displays fearful behaviour. Crucially, this holds true even if the animal has not yet received any kind of (planned) stimulus exposure and training.

Now, one could object that this is inapplicable to humans. After all, many people seem at peace with their surroundings. Peterson would no doubt agree. However, he maintains that '[w]e are protected from such conflict—from subjugation to instinctive terror—by the historical compilation of adaptive information generated in the course of previous novelty-driven exploration' (1999, p. 53). In a way, we are all free riders, since we have each been pulled out of the primordial 'blooming, buzzing confusion' (James 2007, p. 462) of early life by our genes and our parents. The contribution of our surrounding culture to this peace of mind should not be downplayed. By learning a language, for example, we have each imposed a considerable measure of order onto what would have other-wise been a disorderly world. When we learn a word such as 'water', we do not just learn to parrot a sound. Rather, we learn to pick out some liquids and not others. The tedious work of figuring out what to include and what to exclude was done by others, so we benefit from their toil by playing the relevant language game.

Likewise, the maxims and narratives that circulate in our native community predate us. The story of the boy who cried wolf, for example, is a cautionary tale that may have cost some-one's life. As adults, we take all of this for granted. Neverthe-less, Peterson believes there is much to be gained by reminding ourselves that '[w]e are protected from unpredictability by our culturally determined beliefs, by the stories we share' (1999, p.

53). Just as none of us built the hospital or house in which we were born, none of us built the edifice of beliefs that has (hopefully) kept us safe for most of our life. Hence, even when studying personal psychology, the social sciences cannot be dispensed with, because '[s]ocial order is a necessary precondition for psychological stability: it is primarily our companions and their actions (or inactions) that stabilize or destabilize our emotions' (1999, p. 59).

That said, no cultural narrative or constructed housing can ensure total shelter from the world's external influence. The security afforded by well-confirmed maps of meaning and well-constructed spaces nevertheless invites complacency. Peterson, as we saw, thinks that classical behavioural psychology is wrong to regard fear as something learned. Interestingly, Peterson bases his critique on a behaviour that happens before any experiment proper happens. The rat's fearful demeanour upon being placed in a new environment has not been deemed worthy of note, Peterson suggests, because we cannot bring ourselves to accept that life's underlying condition is one of fear. Experimenters are at home in a laboratory, but rats are not. Experimenters therefore 'regard the calm rat as the real rat because we project our misinterpretations of our own habitual nature onto our experimental animals' (1999, p. 59). The comfort afforded by our culture is so pervasive that we forget it is even there. Only the 'odd-ball' intrusion of chaos can goad our attention mechanisms out of their dormant state. Hence, an equivalent of the rat's experience, for humans, would be to tear the roof off a building and expose the researchers to, say, a stormy red Martian sky. They would freak, no learning required.

Antifragility does not make one indestructible. By definition, we can never get used to surprises. We can, however, get used to the idea that this is our basic predicament. Peterson therefore offers a meta-narrative about the natural limits of narratives.

Chapter 3

A world replete with meaning

Peterson is concerned with how humans construct maps of meaning. There is a whole branch of philosophy — semiotics — devoted to studying this (Champagne 2018b). Contemporary semiotic theory instructs us that, fundamentally, there are three ways we come to know the world.

One of them is by linguistic description. If we imbue certain symbols, such as words, with codified significations, we can combine those symbols in a way that captures the properties of some thing, state of affairs, or event. I can tell you, for instance, that a given electrical appliance has certain dimensions, performs certain functions, and has a certain appearance, and these descriptions can give you some appreciation of the appliance in question. Such descriptions are useful because they do not require the presence of the thing described. Indeed, the whole point of describing the electrical appliance is to avoid carrying it with me. Similarly, we can talk of the past, even if it is no longer here. This is an incredible cognitive feat. The flip side, however, is that we can construct descriptions that are not satisfied by any particular thing in the world. I can describe a unicorn, for example, even though no such animal exists. We can lie.

Scientific inquiry thus requires the use of another kind of sign, known as an index. An indexical sign is one that depends on the presence of its object in order to convey its meaning. If, for instance, one writes 'Do not touch' on a sticky label, the linguistic formulation will convey its command to whoever masters the relevant language, but the question of *what* not to touch will depend on where the label is placed. Similarly, dinosaurs are not here now, but their fossils are. Perception involves some form of indexicality, since it requires actual exposure to the stimulus. We would like to think that we can recreate the experience of a hue such as orange merely by imagining it, but really we must open our eyes before the actual colour in order to experience it. Certainly, to acquire the colour concept for the first time, at least one indexical encounter is needed. So to prove that real organisms match the description of unicorns, we would require at least one (live or dead) specimen before us.

While linguistic constructs can be detached from reality, they can nonetheless be anchored to facts by augmenting descriptions with some form of causal contact. The classic example of a causality-based sign is a thermometer. If the volume of the expanding mercury tells us about the ambient temperature, it is because that volume is causally linked to the temperature in a way that is independent of any mind. Of course, to take advantage of the significance afforded by this mind-independent relation, it has to be interpreted. But crucially, this interpretation will be directed at a relation that pre-exists it (and that would continue to hold, even when not interpreted), in the same way that a Post-It note stuck to an object will tell me that it pertains to that object, even when it is written in a language that I don't understand.

The third way we get to know things is by similarity. Just as causation-based indices work differently than convention-based symbols, similarity-based icons work in a way that is unique to this class of signs. When I first see something, the experience lets me have two insights. First, I get a confirmation—visual in this case—that such a thing exists. Second, I get an automatic sense of what other things similar to it would look like. This second insight is not as tangible as the first, since it tells me only that a similar thing *could* exist. Still, nothing is so unique that it is completely unrepeatable, so our experience includes not just codified associations such as words, and causal encounters such as hard evidence, but also latent relations of sameness.

Relations of sameness are particularly important for Peterson because those relations are the basic building blocks of metaphors, which are, in turn, the basic building blocks of narratives. The world is replete with similarity relations, so we can use some of these similarities to increase our knowledge. As Peterson explains:

> Two or more objects or situations come to occupy the same mythological or categorical space [...] because they share similar form, function or capacity to induce affect and compel behavior. A mandrake root, for example, has the nature of a man, symbolically speaking, because it has the *shape* of a man; Mars is a war-like planet because it is red, and red, the color of blood, is associated indelibly with aggression; the metal mercury (and the 'spirit' that inhabits it) is akin to seawater because both may serve as solvents or agents of transformation; the dark and the animal of the forest are the same, because they are both unfamiliar— because they both inhibit ongoing behavior, when they make their appearance; because they both cause *fear*. Metaphor links thing to thing, situation to situation, con- centrating on the phenomenological, affective, functional and motivational features the linked situations share. (Peterson 1999, p. 137)

Peterson's maps of meaning thus make use of the full semiotic repertoire of convention-based symbols (like words), causality- based indices (like thermometers), and similarity-based icons (like metaphors). The channels that convey meaning must interact, since none can work independently. For instance, the metaphors described by Peterson are partly dependent on convention. It is not obvious, say, why a tiny red dot in the night sky should be associated with any human activity such as war. Still, given that there are rudimentary similarities (via a shared colour, in this case), the relations can be used in our attempts to make sense of things.

Of course, as we get better at devising tests and instruments to check our descriptions against hard evidence, our trust in causality-based signs increases while our trust in similarity-based signs decreases. The human-like shape of a mandrake root is a very poor reason to infer its medicinal applicability to humans. Such a claim can now be shown to be false. Likewise, we know that thunder is caused by static electricity generated by the collision of water particles in a gaseous state, so the suggestion that thunder is caused by a man in the sky who strikes a hammer is laughable. We have ample reason to reject a posit such as Thor. Even so, failed hypotheses are how we got to where we are today, so 'in point of epistemological footing the physical objects and the gods differ only in degree and not in kind' (Quine 1961, p. 44).

Importantly, biological evolution has not caught up with scientific advances, so our brains are still hardwired to view the world as a place replete with metaphorical significance. We know Thor does not cause thunder, but we can still be tempted to think that way. Similarly, when we contemplate a region of reality that we have yet to penetrate scientifically, we project our hopes and fears onto the unknown (science fiction narratives being the prime example). Accurately mapping out parts of the world is an accomplishment never finished once and for all, so '[t]he process of metaphorical representation provides a bridge—and an increasingly communicable bridge—between what can be directly explored, experienced and "comprehended", and what remains eternally unknown' (Peterson 1999, p. 137).

As we have seen, linguistic descriptions can be strung together in an intelligible manner, even if no real object matches what they describe. This relative independence from the world is both good and bad. It is bad because it requires us to check, using indices, whether the world in fact includes the thing(s) we describe. Yet language's relative independence from the world is also good, since it allows us to craft mythical and literary narratives about ideal persons and situations that would otherwise never be encountered. A heroic figure such as Wonder Woman may not exist, but contemplating descriptions of her character and actions allows us to hone our sense of what it means to be honourable. Hence, humans need descriptions of the world not just as it is, but also as it could be. This makes the world meaningful.

Viewed in this light, religions supply us not with idols, but with ideals. Peterson holds that '[b]elief has to be grounded in faith' (1999, p. 92), but given that religious narratives were selected for by evolutionary pressures, '[t]here is no reason [...] why such faith cannot be informed, and critically assessed' (1999, p. 92). In that respect, Peterson seems to heed Bonhoeffer's advice that '[w]hen we speak of God in a non-religious way, we must not gloss over the ungodliness of the world, but expose it in a new light' (Bonhoeffer 1959, p. 167). Peterson thinks the best way to conduct such a reassessment is to look for constants that emerge when comparing diverse myths and stories. Following Carl Jung, Peterson calls these constants *archetypes*.

As he explains, 'Jung believed that many complexes had an archetypal (or universal) basis, rooted in biology, and that this rooting had something specifically to do with memory' (Peterson 1999, p. 98). Peterson is aware that Jung's main means of accounting for such memory, the collective uncon-scious, 'appears insufficiently elaborated, from the modern empirical perspective' (1999, p. 92). However, what we find in Peterson's writings is different from what we find in Jung's writings. That is because, in contrast with Peterson, 'Jung was silent on the role of natural selection in the shaping of archetypes. We know that he possessed books by both [Charles] Darwin and Herbert Spencer [...]. However, we can only speculate on the extent to which he was knowledgeable of the specifics of evolutionary theory that were in print during his career' (Walters 1994, p. 294). Peterson tries to update Jung's account in light of what we now know of evolutionary processes.

Evolution works, but it does not work the way we intuitively expect it to. Suppose, for instance, that I am a great golfer. Part of my success in this sport can be explained by my genes, while another part can be explained by my upbringing and learning. We cannot divide what I owe to each source, but we know quite well that these two sources account for who I am right now. Nature and culture nevertheless contribute very differently to a current state of affairs. One can pass one's genes to one's child, but one cannot pass one's upbringing and learning. Or, to be more precise, if parents or guardians pass on their upbringing and learning, it is by repeating in their household the environmental conditions to which they were exposed. Hence, if one's success as a golfer gives one's child a head start because of heredity, the child still must acquire, on her own, the fine motor skills and muscle tissue required.

Storytellers can teach new generations about heroes, just as coaches can teach new generations how to swing a golf club. But no matter how hard we try, the knowledge we acquire by reading books and talking to fellow humans will not get encoded in human eggs or sperm. This poses a problem for archetypes, since they seem to replicate by learning, not genes. 'How can the *fact* of patterned stories—archetypal stories, if you will—be reconciled with the apparent *impossibility* of inherited memory content?' (Peterson 1999, p. 92). Peterson's way out of this is to employ the flexible concept of pattern. Human behaviours aggregate to form large-scale patterns. When you act like a hero, you are 'being heroic', and this is something others before you have done. Likewise, when you act like a coward, you are 'being cowardly', and this is also something others before you have done. Now, let us assume that some behavioural patterns, such as heroism, are conducive to life, flourishing, and the welfare of everyone, whereas other patterns, such as cowardliness, are not. Patterns that have a negative or positive impact on our lives clearly benefit from being known.

In a 2018 conversation with Susan Blackmore, Peterson suggested that the notion of 'meme', suitably adapted, can rescue the embattled notion of archetype. As Richard Dawkins (the originator of the meme concept) put it: 'Darwin's "survival of the fittest" is really a special case of a more general law of *survival of the stable*' (2006b, p. 12). Stability can be found in nature and culture alike. Hence, an archetype, according to Peterson, is nothing but a very large pattern of patterns. He thus holds that 'the longer a feature has existed the more time it has had to be selected—and to shape life. It does not matter whether that feature is physical and biological, or social and cultural. All that matters, from a Darwinian perspective, is permanence' (Peterson 2018a, p. 14). If this is right, then recurring metaphors are amenable to an evolutionary analysis.

Consider the mother/father distinction, which Peterson claims is the base of many myths and metaphors. An infant needs to recognize the people most likely to provide it with nourishment and protection. Nature clearly selected for that, so the distinction has been around for a long time. If one already has a successful handle on the concepts of mother and father, why not use those same concepts to make sense of the unknown and the known? Peterson holds that 'consciousness as a phenomena [*sic*] depends in large part on activation of the ancient circuitry designed for response to the unknown' (1999,

p. 301). According to him, the elementary distinction between mother and father was eventually co-opted for assorted uses that differ from the original one. Thus, at the risk of being speculative, he catalogues the various symbolic associations humans have used (and continue to use) to make sense of their experiences:

> The *unknown* is unexplored territory, nature, the uncon-scious, dionysian [*sic*] force, the *id*, the Great Mother goddess, the queen, the matrix, the matriarch, the container, the object to be fertilized, the source of all things, the strange, the unconscious [*sic*, redundancy in the original], the sensual, the foreigner, the place of return and rest, the maw of the earth, the belly of the beast, the dragon, the evil stepmother, the deep, the fecund, the pregnant, the valley, the cleft, the cave, hell, death and the grave, the moon (ruler of the night and the mysterious dark), uncontrollable emotion, matter and the earth. [...] The *known* is explored territory, culture, Appollinian [*sic*] control, superego, the conscience, the rational, the king, the patriarch, the wise old man and the tyrant, the giant, the ogre, the cyclops, order and authority and the crushing weight of tradition, dogma, the day sky, the countryman, the island, the heights, the ancestral spirits, and the activity of the dead. (Peterson 1999, pp. 103–04)

Critics who accuse Peterson of furthering gender stereotypes rarely attend to the theoretical reasons behind his interest. Peterson's account of cultural patterns draws on what evolu-tionary theorists call 'exaptation'. Whereas an adaptation is 'any feature that promotes fitness and was built by selection for its current role', exaptations are features that 'are fit for their current role' but 'were not designed for it' (Gould and Vrba 1982, p. 6). The patterns that human brains store are not just there to help us cope with the situations that gave rise to those patterns, but also to help us devise new schemes of interpretation when we face novel situations. For example, if you know enough to never turn your back on an animal predator, then treating a human enemy as a 'predator' will let you transpose the lessons learned from one domain to another and infer that you should never turn your back on an enemy. No need to learn that lesson twice. Metaphors thus have a misunderstood cognitive utility.

In any event, the gendered categories studied by Peterson are complicated by the fact that early humans not only used the concepts of mother and father to make sense of the unknown and the known, they also used the concept of the child to make sense of the constant mediation between the two: 'The *knower* is the creative explorer, the ego, the I, the eye, the phallus, the plow, the subject, consciousness, the illuminated or *enlightened* one, the trickster, the fool, the hero, the coward; spirit (as opposed to matter, as opposed to dogma); the sun, son of the unknown and the known (son of the Great Mother and the Great Father)' (1999, pp. 103–04). It would therefore be wrong to describe the worldview painted by Peterson as dualist. The individual hero is the person who knows when to try something new and when to cling to the tried, tested, and true.

Biology influences the content of many narratives, as is the case with our innate fear of serpentine figures (Peterson 1999, pp. 300–01; see Isbell 2009) or our admiration of successful members of our species (Peterson 1999, p. 76). Yet narratives can affect biology too, as is the case when our lifespan increases due to emulating hygienic practices, or when our health improves due to emulating athletic role models. Archetypes grow out of this ever-evolving mixture of learned patterns and innate hardwiring. They fit in neither an innate biological model nor a learned behavioural model, since they mediate between the two. This, at any rate, is the lesson we should draw from Peterson's work on archetypes. Pay attention to only

culture, or only nature, and you are sure to miss or mis-
understand the utility of archetypal depictions.

Nature can be slow to change. My eyes, for instance, will
simply never catch up with the high-focus demands of my
writing career. Culture can also fall behind sudden changes in
biology. One illustration of this comes from the birth control
pill, which gave women unprecedented mastery of their
reproductive system. According to Peterson, the advent of this
contraceptive method dramatically altered the time frames that
govern relationships between men and women. Many couples
understandably took advantage of this new possibility, but
culture has been unable to match this rapid rate of biological
change. The archetypal mother is an image so deeply ingrained
in our psyche that it shows up in primordial mental states, like
dreams. Novels and movies have produced scattered social
representations of women who forego or postpone the general
life-plan of motherhood. However, from an archetypal standpoint, it is unclear what a woman on the pill looks like.
Peterson contends that many myths 'constitute what we know
about our knowing how, before we can state, explicitly, what it
is that we know how' (1999, p. 75). To the extent that
archetypes are our first line of defence when trying to grapple
with the unknown, a woman taking contraceptives cannot turn
to any deep-seated pattern in order to make deep sense of her
choice.

Despite Peterson's chosen example, his account is not
limited to women. Jung, from whom Peterson takes the concept
of archetype, 'believed that the mind was not a blank slate but
prepared before birth to cognitively and emotionally guide the
individual in dealing with certain life situations that are pan-
human' (Walters 1994, p. 290). For instance, my father had a
father, who had a father, and so on. Hence, as a male who has
taken on that iterated paternal role, I am arguably equipped,
biologically and culturally, to confront this challenging
function. Now, suppose that I clone myself. How should I

conceive of my clone—as a brother or a son? We simply do not have the relevant archetype to make sense of this unprecedented experience.

Most of us are aware that our bodies are not endlessly pliable. Likewise, in social matters, we simply cannot do whatever we want. This fact is obscured by the arbitrary character of language. The fictional character Humpty Dumpty famously said that when he uses a word, 'it means just what I choose it to mean'. A person is certainly free to utter what they want. That said, a person is not actually free to decide whether their approach to make words mean different things will gel with the surrounding established patterns. Similarly, going to work in a clown outfit will not violate the laws of physics. However, this deviation from established behaviour is liable to receive the same attention as the 'odd-ball' tone standing out from an otherwise predictable sequence of sounds (see the experiment recounted in Peterson 1999, p. 50). This heightened awareness is not because our co-workers are close minded (although they might be), but rather because the 'characterization of the environment as unknown/known (nature/culture, foreign/familiar) might be regarded as more "fundamental" than any objective characterization' (1999, p. 48).

The hallmark of order is predictability. In fact, we seek order precisely for this epistemological feature. So to the extent that our bodies and cultures have adapted to maximize predictability, our bodies and cultures come with expectations. The merit of these expectations can certainly be called into question—Peterson (1999, p. 34) would never endorse the fallacious inference that goes from 'X has been happening for a long time' to 'X is right'. Even so, collective patterns of behaviour form a more or less stable system—stable enough, at any rate, to have survived this long. Hence, when we zoom out to consider human history in its entirety, prudence emerges as an important virtue. Situating current events on an elongated timeline therefore changes how we view those events (for a survey of hot topics, see Stamos 2008). This is one of the pillars of Peterson's evolutionary methodology.

Someone accustomed to 'blank slate' explanations of social phenomena might be tempted to read determinism into Peterson's stance. However, such a gloss would fail to explain an important datum, namely the very existence of his corpus. Indeed, Peterson wrote *Maps of Meaning* with the express intent of averting world wars. Clearly, his writing and online activism rest on the assumption that improving our lot is sometimes possible and desirable. Why become a clinical psychologist and a vocal public intellectual if people are fated to stay as they are? Despite his desire to improve the world, Peterson insists that to be viable a given plan of action must take into consideration the full map of reality, which includes the individual, their culture, and the natural environment that this culture responds to (1999, p. 136). As a result, social reforms cannot disregard millennia of biological adaptations.

Some are trying to erase biology from classroom discussions of sex, gender, and sexuality (Heying 2017; Champagne 2016c). However, Peterson thinks that, over time, neglecting the biological roots of culture will 'generate a state of affairs [...] that we will come in the decades to follow to deeply and profoundly regret' (2019a). We are free to adopt novel norms and practices, but we are not free to escape our embodiment and all that it entails. Reproductive urges, personality profiles, and other ingrained patterns are not (yet?) things that can be wished away or redirected on a whim. We can try to move away from them, but not only do they exert a centripetal pull — there are good evolutionary reasons to think that this pull is to our benefit. Although it is not always easy to grasp how our free will, innate nature, and acquired culture(s) intermingle, it can be profitable to view Peterson as heeding Francis Bacon's insight that 'nature is only to be commanded by obeying her' (1902, p. 106).

Chapter 4

Using, not misusing, one's brain organ

According to Peterson, the scientific mindset misinterprets ancient myths when it glosses them over as false descriptions of the world, since they are in fact normative blueprints of how to *act*. Natural selection equipped humans with big brains not so they could be better spectators, but so they could be better agents. Hence, '[w]e *may* construct models of "objective reality", and it is no doubt useful to do so. We *must* model meanings, however, in order to survive' (Peterson 1999, p. 22).

It is not mandatory, for example, to know that the molecular structure of water is H_2O. It is mandatory, however, to find water refreshing (and thus worth seeking). The deleterious effects of skipping on water will make themselves known with far more urgency than the deleterious effects of skipping chemistry classes. That is why Peterson defines reality not as a sum of matter but as 'that which selects'. Evolutionary pressures have thus made sure that, from a first-person perspective, the refreshing character of water is more obvious to us than its chemical structure (which can be accessed only with sophisticated instruments). One consequence of this is that in our ordinary practical engagements with things, 'what something signifies is more or less inextricably *part* of the thing, part of its magic' (1999, p. 2). Instead of thinking that water-is-good-because-it-furthers-my-chosen-ends, it is much simpler to think that water-is-good.

Peterson acknowledges that '[i]t was the great feat of science to strip *affect* from *perception*', but he insists that 'the affects generated by experiences are *real*, as well' (1999, p. 4). Because narratives take the world to be teeming with meaning, they are hard to reconcile with standard scientific explanations. The main question we ask of a story is not 'Is it true?' but rather 'Is it any good?' Once we embed stories into a goal-directed conception of life, we can take any candidate story and ask whether it serves our ends. Assuming that one seeks to flourish, a story will be good when its interpretation fosters flourishing and bad when it hinders flourishing.

Mature humans learn to insert some reflective distance between their natural responses and their considered judgments, thereby allowing them to appreciate the mind-independence of the material world. Chemistry is, after all, a perfectly legitimate field of inquiry. Even so, the child-like view that reifies valuations is not one that we can ever completely rid ourselves of—if for no other reason than that it conditions our unthinking reflexes. Peterson, who is a student of Jean Piaget's (1970) developmental theory of knowledge, never loses sight of the stages where higher cognitive skills take root. We can overwrite our earliest stories, but they leave a residual trace on all our maps.

Interestingly, mastering social situations seems to have been more important, from an evolutionary standpoint, than mastering logic. Take, for instance, conditional propositions. These propositions have an asymmetric 'if… then…' structure that allows one to make some inferences and not others. To illustrate, suppose that one is told, 'If the roads are fixed, then the economy will improve.' Now suppose that, as a matter of fact, 'The roads are not fixed.' Can one conclude from these two propositions taken jointly that the economy will not improve? This conclusion is not logically supported by the propositions.

Most people are bad at figuring this out. However, landmark experiments (by Cosmides and Tooby 1992) have shown that when an if–then proposition involves a promise, our inferential ability spikes upward. For instance, suppose I make the following promise before a crowd of witnesses: 'If the sports team wins, then I will shave my head.' The team, it turns out, does not win. What will my head look like the next day? We can give this inference a jolt of psychological intuition by asking: would seeing me with a full head of hair (i.e. not shaved) allow you to call me a liar? That certainly would not follow. The logical structure is the same as the previous if–then inference about paved roads. But calling someone a liar is a big deal, so we are good logicians when it comes to promises. We had to be — otherwise the web of trust that holds together our social relationships would have unravelled long ago. Ethics thus predates logic, both historically and individually.

According to Peterson, this need to negotiate between our early and late ways of organizing experience helps to explain the persistent influence of myths and fictions. Humans can distinguish heroes from villains simply by their actions, without forming a definition of heroism and villainy. As the psychologist Jerome Bruner (2004) remarks, children understand stories long before they understand arguments. A popular internet meme like 'What would Batman do?' is thus a massive ethical tome, subjected to maximal informational compression.

Despite our considerable scientific and technological advances, we need to immerse ourselves in a fictional world where people and events display the various values that we orient ourselves by, especially when we do not know how to self-consciously articulate those values. 'The automatic attribution of meaning to things — or the failure to distinguish between them initially — is a characteristic of narrative, of myth, not of scientific thought. Narrative accurately captures the nature of raw experience. Things *are* scary, people *are* irritating, events *are* promising, food *is* satisfying—at least in terms of our basic experience' (Peterson 1999, p. 2).

Peterson remarks that '[i]t has taken centuries of firm discipline and intellectual training, religious, proto-scientific, and scientific [...] to produce a mind that regards *real* as something separable from *relevant*' (1999, p. 3). Ridding the official scientific worldview of all values did not make values disappear. All it did was generate a gap. Although we can 'brilliantly manipulate the thing', this technical prowess has not stopped us from being 'victims [...] of the uncomprehended emotions generated by [...] the thing' (1999, p. 5). Peterson believes that humankind can no longer tolerate a discrepancy between its descriptive mastery of the material world and its relative ignorance of ethical matters. As a teenager visiting a Cold War missile silo, Peterson 'couldn't understand how belief systems could be so important to people that they were willing to risk the destruction of the world to protect them' (2018a, p. xxx). Our brains are great at knowing the laws that govern the natural world, but this incredible evolutionary adaptation now proves supremely maladaptive. Tribalism, it turns out, does not mix well with subatomic physics.

If the end point of a belief or belief system is a nuclear mushroom, we clearly need to orient ourselves toward a better end. Part of Peterson's appeal is that he articulates the widespread sentiment that what the world needs right now is not more science, but more wisdom. It is too late, though, to believe in religious worldviews without qualification, since '[o]ur constant cross-cultural interchanges and our capacity for critical reasoning has undermined our faith in the traditions of our forebears—perhaps for good reason' (Peterson 1999, pp. 10–11). Peterson might therefore be classified as endorsing what Richard Kearney (2011) calls 'anatheism', the (successful or unsuccessful) attempt to return to God after God's demise. Peterson thinks that humans should satisfy their ingrained craving for religious guidance, because 'the individual cannot live without belief — without action and valuation — and science cannot provide that belief' (1999, p. 11). However, the responsible thing to do is to reinstate such beliefs carefully, updating our appreciation of their normative power.

We see, then, that Peterson's reflex is not utopian but historical. Instead of looking to the future and crafting a world-view from scratch, he enjoins us to look to past narratives so as to recapture insights that have a proven track record. As Peterson sees it, this strategy is preferable for a variety of reasons. First, we cannot escape history. Since any utopian scheme has no doubt been tried before, we should learn from failed attempts at radical social reform. We cannot foresee all the flaws of an idea simply by thinking harder about it, so we should privilege ideas that have encountered genuine adversity over time. The hubris of presenting one's generation as the culmination of world history has been at the root of some of the bloodiest massacres ever witnessed. The 'great rationalist ideologies, after all — fascist, say, or communist — demonstrated their essential uselessness within the space of mere genera-tions', but '[t]raditional societies, predicated on religious notions, have survived — essentially unchanged, in some cases, for tens of thousands of years' (Peterson 1999, p. 8). The main lesson of history is that we should learn from history.

When we study history, we find that '[p]rior to the time of Descartes, Bacon and Newton, man lived in an animated, spiritual world, saturated with meaning, imbued with moral purpose. The nature of this purpose was revealed in the stories people told each other — stories about the structure of the cosmos and the place of man' (Peterson 1999, p. 5). Peterson does not advocate a return to such pre-science and pre-enlightenment worldviews. He does, however, note that the average person who lived before these intellectual sea changes 'was certainly not plagued by the plethora of rational doubts and moral uncertainties that beset his modern counterpart' (1999, p. 5). Peterson's view is reminiscent of John McDowell's.

According to McDowell, ancient Greek texts reveal a conception where humans' 'rationality is integrally part of their animal nature, and the conception is neither naturalistic in the modern sense [...] nor fraught with philosophical anxiety. What makes this possible is that' Greek thinkers like Aristotle are 'innocent of the very idea that nature is the realm of law and therefore not the home of meaning' (McDowell 2002, p. 109).

The rapid rise of modern science eclipsed such value-laden worldviews. Even so, Peterson contends that mythical narratives are able to capture something that scientific descriptions cannot. Whereas science specifies 'the most effective mode of reaching an end (given a defined end)', myths offer a more or less systematic 'description of the world as it *signifies* (for *action*)' (Peterson 1999, p. 9). Since an organism is more interested in what a thing means (for it) than what a thing is (in itself), myths prove invaluable. Peterson's account thus predicts that if people are forced to choose between mythical meaning and scientific truth, they will on average prefer the former.

Naturally, ridding oneself of the most effective mode of reaching an end is not to one's advantage. Peterson's complaint is that, all too often, those who promote science set up such a forced choice. Hence, as scientific accounts rose in well-deserved prominence, myths and other fictional narratives began to play a decreasing role in guiding our lives. In Peterson's view, we hastily discarded our most lasting stories because we overlooked their evolutionary utility. It took a while for the notion of evolution to embed itself into our deliberative give and take, and longer still for scholars to see how evolutionary principles could shed light on cultural phenomena. The story-free explanation of the world was thus able to thrive for about a century or two without any serious opposition. Peterson nevertheless thinks it is time to reinstate narrative patterns as genuine instruments in the human quest for survival and well-being. 'This turn to the mythic way of knowing by Peterson and many others is not meant to under-mine the scientific way of knowing. Instead, it is merely meant to correct an obvious historic imbalance in ways of seeing and being' (Dart 2020, p. 69).

Adherence to scientism did not eradicate the guidance of myths in our lives; it merely drove that guidance underground. Hence, Peterson does not have to reinstate the age-old insights contained in myths and religious texts, since '[t]he fundamental tenets of the Judeo-Christian moral tradition continue to govern every aspect of the actual individual behavior and basic values of the typical Westerner [...]. He neither kills, nor steals (or, if he does, he hides his actions, even from his own aware-ness), and he tends, in theory, to treat his neighbor as himself' (1999, p. 6). Despite being unacknowledged in the official scientific worldview, traditional values continue to be operative at psychological and social levels.

We can, if we wish, continue this discrepant bookkeeping, but doing so exerts a personal and collective cost. On a per-sonal level, leading a bifurcated life means that 'our integrity has vanished' (Peterson 1999, p. 7). When we act only 'as if' values exist, we give ourselves the means to escape the demands of moral integrity when the going gets tough. Why not cheat on a partner if the world is just a collision of particles? On a collective scale, seeing moral claims as massive errors means going against the Darwinian inference that the age of a trait predicts its utility (even when we do not quite know how to convincingly reconstruct this utility). Nature tends to shave off anything that does not serve a function, so '[h]ow is it that complex and admirable ancient civilizations could have developed and flourished, initially, if they were predicated upon nonsense?' (Peterson 1999, p. 7). Error theory (e.g. Mackie 1977) purports to purge the world of mysterious posits, but it turns the survival value of moral convictions into a mystery. The persistence of moral structures and strictures therefore needs to be explained, not explained away:

> Our behavior is shaped (at least in the ideal) by the same
> mythic rules — *thou shalt not kill, thou shalt not covet* — that
> guided our ancestors, for the thousands of years they lived
> without benefit of formal empirical thought. This means
> that those rules are so powerful — so necessary, at least —
> that they maintain their existence (and expand their
> domain) even in the presence of explicit theories that under-
> mine their validity. [...] Is it not likely that this indicates
> modern philosophical ignorance, rather than ancestral
> philosophical error? (Peterson 1999, pp. 7–8)

Peterson's main grievance against the 'New Atheism' of Sam
Harris (2004), Daniel Dennett (2006), and Richard Dawkins
(2006a) is that it inverts the order of experiential priority. The
disenchanted conception of the world as comprised of
extended material things is not one that humans can actually
believe in. It is not clear that this materialist conception of the
world is even true (see Champagne 2013). We are organisms
with needs, and those needs colour everything that comes
within our ken. Peterson would agree with Hilary Putnam
(2002) that we value truth and that assessments of value
inevitably get entangled with assessments of truth or falsity.
Peterson believes that if natural science consistently followed
through with this realization, it would not be business as usual.
If nothing else, evolutionary biology would become more
fundamental than physics — at least if 'fundamentality' is taken
as tracking orders of logical dependence, not relative scale.

  Understanding this inversion can help to explain Peterson's
much-discussed disagreement with Harris (in the latter's
Making Sense podcast, number 62). In a bid to put the
descriptive (material) world squarely ahead of the normative
(experiential) world, Harris presents Peterson with the following scenario. Imagine a world where all humans vanish as a
result of nuclear self-annihilation. Harris contends that in such
a world, truths about nuclear fission would retain their status

as true, despite the conclusive evidence that those truths proved detrimental to human survival, writ large. Peterson disagrees. As he puts it, the destruction of our species would show that our knowledge of nuclear facts was 'not true enough'.

In saying this, Peterson is essentially working from a different conception than Harris, who conceives of the truth as a correspondence between a claim and a fact. Yet one can also construe truth as what suitably equipped, honest inquirers would agree on at the end of inquiry (see Legg 2014). Since we are ignorant and flawed, truth is not what we know now but rather the limit of what we could know. According to Peterson, this convergence theory of truth presupposes the presence of inquirers at the end of inquiry. Knowledge is thus inextricably linked with the continued survival of knowers.

The function of the brain organ is to know. However, organs are embedded in organisms, so in the grand scheme of things our brains are not there primarily to know but rather to help us live. The same could be said of kidneys. These organs are not there primarily to filter blood but rather to assist with nutrition and thus survival. In his discussions of epistemological questions, Peterson never forgets that human intelligence serves a specific purpose, namely the continuation of life amid a hostile and ever-changing environment. Since the activity of thinking is not an end in itself, we can take any product of our evolved intelligence and evaluate whether it serves or hinders the ultimate goal of life.

Peterson does not believe that one can do this evaluation in isolation. It would make matters simpler if we could take an isolated claim and check whether it matches or mismatches with some isolated fact in the world. It is doubtful, however, that such piecemeal correspondence relations can be had (see Quine 1961, pp. 20–46). This is because the truth of a given claim can change as the range of context changes.

To see this, consider the following question (borrowed from Brett and Eric Weinstein): are whales fish? If we consider only rough-and-ready traits that can be observed by ordinary means —from the deck of a boat, say—the answer seems to be yes. They spend their lifetime swimming in water, have the general body shape of a fish, eat other small fish at sea, and so on. Yet if we compare whales to other species and engage in a more systematic taxonomic effort, we eventually glean that whales possess the defining characteristics not of fish, but of mammals. They have lungs, not gills; they breathe air, not water; the females give birth to live young instead of releasing unfertilized eggs; they provide milk; and so on. Now that we have enlarged the context, the answer changes: whales are not fish. Most folks stop there. But if we keep zooming out, the answer can revert back to a yes. This is because the first whales evolved from a terrestrial or land-dwelling ancestor about 50 million years ago, but all terrestrial life initially sprang from the sea.

The moral to be learned from this example is that as the timeline under consideration stretches, our evaluation of a claim's truth may change. The initial claim that 'Whales are fish' went from being true (when we considered only ordinary knowledge), to false (when we considered scientific knowledge), to true (when we considered scientific knowledge across a much longer span of time). Now, what happens when you zoom out as far as you can and take a fresh look at things such as smartphones and internet porn? Clearly, the truth of the claim 'These things are good for you' is capable of changing, depending on the context. Peterson's methodological recommendation is to adopt as wide a context as we can, since life itself began adapting to environmental pressures long before the current crop of individuals were born.

Nature has given us brains to help us survive, but that clever grey organ can be misused in ways that undermine our survival. As Peterson explains, '[t]he incautious, imaginative (and resentful) can easily use their gift of socially constructed intelligence to undermine moral principles that took eons to generate and that exist for valid but invisible reasons' (1999, p. 251).

To better appreciate Peterson's stance, consider the following. Imagine that you are somewhere on the American continent and that you must go to New York. How should you get there? Near you is a man with a car. You ask him whether he could drive you there. He answers that he would be willing to, but he recommends that you instead take the train, which is much faster. Fair enough, you decide to follow his advice and take the train. While waiting to buy tickets at the train station, you meet an entrepreneur who explains to you, in convincing technical detail, how the train you intend to take is inferior. Some trains, he continues, now float on a cushion of energy. Combined with an aerodynamic design, this magnetic levitation dramatically reduces friction, which in turn maximizes speed and efficiency. This almost sounds like science fiction, so to back up his claims the entrepreneur offers you a tour of his factory. There, you get to witness first-hand these technological marvels. Truly, magnetic levitation is superior to traditional railway tracks. In fact, it turns out that if the train were to travel in a vacuum, the top speed achieved would be even greater. Hence, engineers are currently busy designing tunnels that will completely eliminate the last remaining source of friction, namely the contact with ambient atmosphere. The question I now want to ask is: would this new tunnel-encased model be better?

Usually, the first reflex is to confirm the data. The internet can be a good source of information. However, because some of the information found online can be flawed or faked, one should also consult experts in the field with the appropriate credentials. Clearly, a rigorous evaluation will, if done correctly, demand a high level of concentration. How would

Peterson assess the question of train design that I have just described?

I have no clue. However, his philosophy would insist on establishing one crucial point: *will the technology in question get you to New York?*

All too often, we get bogged down in so many technical details and sub-distinctions that we lose sight of our ends. Those who uncritically privilege analysis over synthesis are especially prone to this. Zooming in closer is sometimes important, but once we are done we have to see whether and how our results fit in a bigger whole (see Sciabarra 2000). Peterson holds that since our brains are there to serve us, we cannot assess the merit of anything unless we can connect that thing back to the task of staying alive. In the scenario just described, you need to go to New York, but presumably there was a reason for this too. Not every situation requires one to give such a full story. Still, Peterson would insist that if the friction-free, high-speed train does *not* get you to your destination, this option will be inferior to the simple car ride you requested at the start.

Does this mean that Peterson is against science and technology? Not at all. His stance simply refuses to give science and technology a free pass. We have evolved to make artefacts, such as jugs, arrows, beds, cars, and nuclear power plants. As fascinating as these human creations are, they possess only instrumental value. Humans are on Earth primarily to live, not to know. Naturally, living well requires knowing much. But we run into all sorts of misguided consequences whenever we invert the order of priority.

Chapter 5

The roots of morality in personality types and early social interactions

Peterson was trained as a psychologist, his favourite topic is religion, and he is best known for his comments on politics. What, one might wonder, can these disparate fields possibly have in common? One concept that skewers all of them is personality.

Peterson has co-authored empirical studies on the link between personality types and political orientation (e.g. Tritt, Inzlicht and Peterson 2013; Xu and Peterson 2017; Xu, Mar and Peterson 2013), as well as on the link between political orientation and happiness or well-being (Burton, Plaksa and Peterson 2015). Studies have shown that a preoccupation with religious institutions and formal belief systems tends to be associated with political 'conservatism', whereas a preoccupation with spirituality and the subjective experience of the sacred is associated with political 'liberalism'. Interest in organized religion and spirituality go hand in hand. But when there is a difference between the two, 'the relative prominence of these dimensions within any given individual appears to be an important predictor of political orientation' (Hirsh, Walberg and Peterson 2013, p. 18).

Peterson thus brings to regular political conversations empirical considerations that few mainstream commentators ever think about. Specifically, he works from the recognition that, as a rule, we often choose our political beliefs because those beliefs resonate with our individual personality profile. For instance, the trait called Agreeableness divides into Politeness and Compassion, but it is 'possible that Compassion would relate to the liberal emphasis on fairness and equality, whereas Politeness would relate to the conservative emphasis on order and traditionalism' (Hirsh, DeYoung, Xu and Peterson 2010, p. 656).

Much of this research is ongoing, so there is healthy disagreement among psychologists about which model is best. Still, it is disturbing to think that humans vote like they pick items in a restaurant menu. The robust correlations unearthed by personality psychology thus pose a problem: how can individuals in a democratic society come to terms with their political differences, if personality traits basically ensure that everyone is already set in their ways?

Clearly, it would be unrealistic to demand or expect that individuals completely overhaul themselves. It would also be silly and simplistic to declare that those who demonstrate one trait more than another are wrong/evil. Since different personality traits all have their worth, Peterson suggests that so long as the channels of conversation are open and people with diverse viewpoints converse in good faith, the truth can prevail. If this sounds naïve, consider the alternative: if people with certain biases don't get exposed to differing views, those biases will never stand a chance of eventually correcting each other. The non-profit advocacy group Heterodox Academy is premised on this very idea:

The surest sign that a community suffers from a deficit of viewpoint diversity is the presence of orthodoxy, most readily apparent when members fear shame, ostracism, or any other form of social retaliation for questioning or challenging a commonly held idea. In these contexts, it is likely that the dominant idea is not entirely correct because it is protected from challenge and change. (heterodoxacademy.org, accessed in early 2019; this statement has since been given a more timid wording)

We cannot eradicate the biases that come with personality profiles. We can, however, structure institutions (such as universities) so that the various biases balance each other out. Those who privilege 'chaos' neglect some aspects of the truth, as do those who privilege 'order' (Peterson 1999, p. 339). But if we let each make their case, consensus or compromise has a chance to build around the best proposal(s).

Of course, Peterson's fix will appeal only to those who are antifragile enough to work alongside folks who don't always confirm their beliefs.

Why is it that some people get along well with others, while others do not? Peterson believes that the rudiments of moral behaviour are acquired in childhood by playing games. Ethics often addresses life-or-death issues, but the games that children play take place in a make-believe space sheltered from real-life consequences. Many animals learn rudimentary hunting skills from simulated fights with their siblings. Humans do the same, Peterson suggests, only they eventually convert what they have learned into oral and written formats.

Peterson agrees with the psychologist Jean Piaget that the various games children play are not just games; rather, the ability to follow rules, which children acquire by playing with other children, is the first draft for what will in time develop into a full-fledged moral code. Importantly, children learn which actions in a game are permitted and forbidden, without being able to say why the actions in question are permitted and forbidden (see Kohlberg 1969). Eventually, children become able to describe the rules they follow. According to Piaget (2013, p. 17), this happens when children are between eleven and twelve years old. Ask a group of eight-year-olds what the rules of marbles are, and they all give different answers. Ask them again four years later, and they all formulate the same set of rules. Young children thus stand in the same relationship to reality that most humans stood before the advent of explicit philosophical reflection on ethics.

To explain this moral learning, Peterson calls on the stages of psychological development catalogued by Piaget. Children start with unstructured play that involves bodily activities such as jumping, running, and throwing. These activities help to develop the basic motor skills that will be needed throughout the child's life. A parent who provides Lego blocks for their infant will notice that, before the age of two, the infant will simply gather and dump those objects. Sometime after two, children start stacking those objects in a way that gives some thought to the resulting structure. This kind of 'adaptation at the sensorimotor level occurs prior to—and lays the groundwork for—the more abstracted forms of adaptation that characterize adulthood' (Peterson 1999, p. 73).

As children start engaging in fantasy and role-playing, they start emulating the people around them. A child might, for example, bring a Lego block to his/her head and speak into it, like a phone. Such playful imitation lets the child act out his or her nascent sense that talking on the phone is seen by others as a valuable activity, even if the child cannot (yet) explain why it is valuable. Peterson thus agrees with Piaget that 'the imitating child in fact *embodies* more information than he "understands" (represents)' (1999, p. 74). In this way, '[a] child can be "good" without being a moral philosopher' (1999, p. 73)—in the same way that adults can conform with the law without being legal scholars.

The range of playable games increases dramatically (in complexity and enjoyment) when other players get incorpora- ted. Once a child reaches this stage, physical objects can be dispensed with. The game of tag, for instance, does not require anything beyond a set of players who follow rudimentary rules. The source of constraint also changes when children start playing primarily with each other instead of with objects. Objects have stable properties (shape, hardness, and so on) that permit or forbid certain moves. A square peg, for example, simply will not enter a round hole. But when the games at hand are primarily social, all that stops possible transgressions is the fact that these moves are frowned upon. Crossing a line in the sand will certainly not violate the laws of physics. The child's peers, though, may take this physical displacement as the violation of a rule.

Violating a rule has consequences. 'During the first stage rules are not yet coercive in character [...] because they are purely motor', but eventually one reaches a stage where 'a rule is looked upon as a law due to mutual consent, which you must respect if you want to be loyal but which it is permissible to alter on the condition of enlisting general opinion on your side' (Piaget 2013, p. 18). Once the child's brain has become adept at tracking the stable properties of physical objects, it begins tracking the more or less stable boundaries that govern the social world.

As one learns to respect social rules habitually, the origin of those rules effaces itself in ordinary experience. Adults, for instance, know not to stand too close to a stranger on the street. Two metres away is fine, but two centimetres makes one a threat. We may not be able to state at what exact distance this change of status occurs, but our habitual mastery of this unwritten rule (which can differ slightly from culture to culture) regulates our everyday behaviour. Peterson suggests that our most strongly held moral intuitions were acquired in a similar way, during our childhood. We may not be able to explain why hitting others is wrong—justifying this principle is harder than it seems—but we know enough not to hit others.

When children join a group, they surrender a part of their autonomy. A child is free to make up any rule she wants, but it is unlikely that others will follow her new rules. Rules, then, are dependent on minds for their existence—this is all that makes the line in the sand a boundary—but rules are independent from any particular mind. Hence, 'individual innovations, just as in the case of language, succeed only when they meet a general need and when they are collectively sanctioned as being in conformity with the "spirit of the game"' (Piaget 2013, p. 13).

Looking at the game of marbles, Piaget thought that it 'contains an extremely complex system of rules, that is to say, a code of laws, a jurisprudence of its own' (2013, p. 1). A game like marbles may be trivial, but striving for success in a game is not. Indeed, children 'aspire from their hearts to the virtue, supremely characteristic of human dignity, which consists in making a correct use of the customary practices of a game' (Piaget 2013, p. 2). The praiseworthy status that can be gained from skilfully mastering a game is a driving engine of human behaviour—think of the social influence that a basketball star can have, for instance. We don't just follow rules; we follow those who follow rules in an exemplary manner.

Peterson is drawn to Piaget's work on game playing because it gives a purely natural account of morality's origins. So long as humans live together, they have no choice but to acquire rule-following skills. Learning to play a game means 1) learning what one can and cannot do and 2) learning to act in accordance with these dos and don'ts. As Piaget rhetorically asks: 'If this is not "morality", then where does morality begin?' (2013, p. 2).

Developmental psychology's account of the origin of values can, Peterson thinks, be reconciled with Darwinian theory. Those who learned to play the game of life well enough to survive passed their knowledge down to their descendants in the form of myths and other action-oriented narratives. The lessons contained in myths and narratives were eventually codified, but those lessons guided humans long before their codification. Seeking revenge with violence, for instance, is a bad game to play, because such a game cannot be sustained. As Aeschylus's *Oresteia* or *The Godfather* movies show us, revenge killings always trigger more revenge killings. In this game, no one wins. Humans have learned this the hard way, from repeated failures and successes in their experiences. The short-term gain but long-term futility of revenge is a fundamental fact about the human condition, so it can be told in any era, in any language.

Stories, especially religious stories, aim to depict the ideal player. The ultimate player, according to Peterson, is the one who wins at the ultimate game, namely life. Since life is the confrontation of suffering and the overcoming of ignorance, we need an ideal of what it means to do those things superbly.

When commenting on political and social affairs, Peterson will often say things like 'I don't think this is a good game to play' or 'that's a much better game for us to play'. He is not implying that political and social affairs should be taken lightly. Rather, he deploys the word 'game' in the quasi-technical sense used by Piaget, indicating a set of (stated or unstated) rules that coordinate human behaviours (compare this with Wittgenstein 2001). Peterson claims that a society's explicit rules (laws, constitution, etc.) grow out of—and derive their everyday authority from—a complex fabric of myths, stories, rituals, and metaphors that humans have been refining for millennia. The purpose of these established narrative patterns is not to enter-tain but to guide action. We need a picture of the world we find ourselves in, plus a set of ideals about how to act. Police officers cannot enforce laws everywhere all the time, so a society works best when, deep down, everybody has a shared sense of what is permissible and what is not. Tradition provides that.

Importantly, tradition can only convey tenets that are replicable in the long run. Some games are better than others. For instance, when regulating mating, consensual sex is better than rape; when regulating the movement of goods and services, trade is better than theft; and so on. According to Peterson, the best game would be one that can be played by everyone in any place forever.

Now, one might worry that such a sustainable game cannot exist, since people, places, and times vary too much. The solution, Peterson suggests, is to make sure that the shared narrative has a sufficiently low resolution. A map of the world that includes specific elements such as lords and ladies, cities and suburbs, kosher and non-kosher foods, black people and white people will clearly fail to command the respect of some people. However, a map that includes universal categories such as parent and child, known and unknown, and consensual and non-consensual acts will have maximum applicability.

Our upbringing ensures that we all have a general picture of the world and the people in it. We have no control over this first draft. As adults, though, we can question whether these deep-seated representations are any good. The crucial choice, according to Peterson, is whether we will treat other people primarily as individuals or as members of groups. This choice is crucial because treating others as individuals yields a viable game, whereas treating others as members of a group yields a game that is bound to collapse.

When one encounters someone whom one does not know, one has two options. On the one hand, one can acknowledge not knowing *this* person and can thereby initiate a process of dialogue and discovery. This is individualism. Getting to know someone on an individual basis is a clear instantiation of Peterson's account of the exchange between chaos and order. The aspects of a person that one does not know represent chaos, the uncertain portions of one's local map. The aspects of a person that one has mapped represent order, since they let one know what to expect of the person. I may have a thorough map of a colleague at work, but there is a whole side of that person that I remain ignorant about, such as how they behave during their leisure time or at home. Encounters with unfamiliar people can be valuable, especially if we assume that the person we are dealing with knows something we don't (Peterson 2018a, pp. 233–56). Yet happy endings are not guaranteed, since a process of dialogue and discovery can also reveal that the person in question is not worthy of one's companionship. Judgments of another person's character are never complete, but they should reflect the best evidence-based picture one can draw. An individualist must therefore stand at the boundary between chaos and order and stay constantly responsive to the evidence obtained.

In a 2014 classroom lecture (Personality Lecture 10), Peterson said, 'I've learned more about listening from [Carl] Rogers than from any other personality theorist or psycho-therapist that I've encountered' (see also Peterson 2018a, pp. 245–48, 253–56). Rogers (1965) was mainly addressing clinicians, but Peterson profitably carries his insights about active listening (Rogers and Farson 1957) over to ordinary conversations, in particular political conversations. Peterson contends that, in those circumstances, listening is 'way more interesting than trying to impose your viewpoint' (Personality Lecture 10). This is because 'people who radically differ […] tell you things that you haven't considered. It doesn't mean you have to agree with them, but it's much more informative to walk away from a conversation having learned something that you didn't know than it is having won the stupid argument — which you can't win anyways' (for a similar view, see Muldoon 2017).

Crucially, one's verdict about a person's merit (or about the merit of their beliefs) is to be rendered, if at all, *after* one has extensively conversed with them, not before. Listening has an ethical component, but it is also the discursive application of two important epistemological principles, namely the respect for evidence (empiricism) and the recognition of one's capacity to err (fallibilism).

The other option is to treat a person as a member of a group. Humans spent most of their prehistory and history in the relative safety of tribes, so the ability to rapidly detect people who are unlike us is with us still. Tapping into this primordial system, one can decide to deal with *that type* of person. This group-based approach reverses the individualist sequence, putting judgment ahead of acquired evidence. Or, more precisely, it bases itself on evidence, just not relevant evidence. After all, one's sight does tell one something about a stranger's physical appearance. Outward appearance can therefore let one drag another person from the realm of chaos into order. Instead of being an unpredictable mixture of known and unknown, the person now becomes a predictable instance of a general pattern (that is learned elsewhere in one's culture). This technique can be applied to politics. 'Justice' can simply be *defined* as 'imitating the demographic pie-chart of society at large'. Using this standard, moral judgments can immediately be rendered (e.g. 'None of the authors on this course syllabus are under five feet tall, therefore this course suppresses the voices of short people' —and so on).

Importantly, this group-based approach does not require any dialogue or inquiry, only a quick glance. Moral clarity is assured, since gauging the degree of match or mismatch with a fixed demographic reference point is relatively easy. Moral confidence is also assured, since nothing I do can ever rid you of your preconceived opinion(s) about me. So instead of dealing with a person who has an unrepeatable personal history and beliefs that escape you, you can deal with, say, 'a mean, mad white man'—to echo a comment made by the sociology professor Michael Eric Dyson (see Dyson *et al.* 2018, pp. 76–77).

This group-based approach may be going viral, but it is not new. Consider the example cited by Peterson (2018b, p. xvi):

> We are not fighting against single individuals. We are exterminating the bourgeoisie as a class. It is not necessary during the interrogation to look for evidence proving that the accused opposed the Soviets by word or action. The first question you should ask him is what class does he belong to, what is his origin, his education and his profession. These are the questions that will determine the fate of the accused. (Martin Latsis, *Red Terror*, November 1, 1918)

As Peterson notes, '[i]t is not as if the boundaries of such a category [of the bourgeoisie] are self-evident, there for the mere perceiving' (2018b, p. xvi). That is why race-based purges are so potent. The approach taken by Dyson links a person to a group based solely on some surface features of their body (skin tones seem paramount, but hair colours ostensibly do not cause any kerfuffle). In a flash, one's outward appearance saddles one with a mix of unearned guilt and unearned merit. A person can be blamed for reprehensible actions that others in the person's alleged group have done, even if the person in question has never done those reprehensible actions. Likewise, a person can take credit for laudable actions that others in the person's alleged group have done, even if the person in question has never done those laudable actions. Since most surface features of the body do not change, nothing one does will ever alter the moral standing that one has been given.

Peterson contends that in the long run this is not a viable game. Since groups usually endure longer than individuals, grievances are allowed to outlast the lifespans of perpetrators. As a result, even when all those who committed a gruesome act have died, descendants of the victims can still claim offence and seek retribution. No amount of actual peace in the present will ever clean the ledger of the past. Peterson thus claims—

quite rightly, I think—that there is no way to take on tribalism without also taking on tribal conflict. By its internal logic, the group-based approach *must* end in a bloodbath. Those seeking lasting peace should therefore look elsewhere than identity politics.

Peterson stresses how difficult it was for humans to realize the importance of the individual. Our first inklings of individualism's promise appeared in myths long before it got canonized in carefully stated political documents such as constitutions. Not every society has succeeded in developing a low-resolution story about itself wherein the individual, not the group, is the basic unit of moral and legal consideration. Even in societies that have developed an individualist outlook, the accomplishment is under constant threat of a tribal revival.

> Western morality and behavior [...] are predicated on the assumption that every individual is sacred. This belief was already extant in its nascent form, among the ancient Egyptians, and provides the very cornerstone of Judeo-Christian civilization. [...] In the absence of this central assumption, the body of Western law—formalized myth, codified morality—erodes and falls. There are no individual rights, no individual value—and the foundation of the Western social (and psychological) structure dissolves. (Peterson 1999, p. 261)

As befits an individualist ethic, the best way to combat this threat of dissolution is not to blame others but to take personal responsibility. Instead of seeing a new person as *that type* of person, you can strive to approach each individual as *this* person—even if doing so means letting go of ready-made formulas that render the person more predictable. The tribal urge to carve the world into various groups is strong, so replacing stereotypes with genuine dialogue requires that one be an 'exploratory communicative hero' (Peterson 1999, p. 241).

As demanding as this stance is, iterated decisions to engage with others as individuals can make all the difference.

'Tag, you're it!' is a game that taggers and tagged might want to play, provided the roles can be switched around. However, 'Tag, you're *forever* it *no matter what!*' is a game that only taggers will want to play. Who gets to decide who will be the taggers? Only naked power play will settle that.

We can, if we want, glance at each other and use disparaging names, based on whatever rapid identifications we have made. But I agree with Peterson that there are better games to play. Like a client who must come to therapy 'actively and voluntarily' (Rogers 1965, p. 7, fn. 1), people unconvinced that the game of identity politics is going nowhere can stay on that merry-go-round for as long as they want. In the meantime, Peterson and others (like myself) are busy building a viable alternative for those who want to dismount.

Chapter 6

The transformative power of speech and individual action

One would have thought that a scholar interested in stories would have little interest in prehistory, the vast span of human time devoid of language. With Peterson, this is not the case. That is because, according to Peterson, humans 'are *primarily* concerned with the affective or emotional significance of the environment. Along with our animal cousins, we devote ourselves to fundamentals: will this (new) thing eat me? Can I eat it? Will it chase me? Should I chase it? Can I mate with it?' (1999, p. 22, for a similar view, see Uexküll 1982, p. 33). Peterson does not limit his study to the written record, because his theory of how we cope with our most vital questions comes in stages, and the first stages are non-verbal.

When we zoom out as far as we can, we see that language arrived on the scene only fairly recently. Peterson thus makes allowances for the fact that '[p]rocedural knowledge develops long before declarative knowledge, in evolution and individual development, and appears represented in "unconscious" form, expressible purely in performance' (1999, p. 73). Body language had to come before verbal language.

Several things had to happen before our earliest ancestors could speak. As apes started to walk upright, their hands became free to perform more delicate tasks. As Peterson explains, '[t]he hand itself was rendered more useful by the development of vertical stance, which extended visual range and freed the upper body from the demands of locomotion' (1999, pp. 64–65). This increased dexterity allowed our ancestors to alter the objects they found on the ground. The evolutionary developments that eventually rewarded mutants who had larger brain sizes were set in motion by adaptations in our appendages, specifically our hands, 'which are capable of an immense number of complex and sophisticated operations' (1999, p. 64). Because of these fortuitous changes in our anatomy, our ancestors no longer had to settle for the lottery of the environment as it stood, since they could now alter that environment.

To turn a rock or branch into something that will serve a desired function—cutting or hitting, say—one must have some rudimentary mental image of what shape that object will have, in advance of actually having it. For instance, one must picture a stone as having a sharp edge, even though it currently has a smooth surface. It is one thing to envision the-world-as-it-is, but quite another to envision the-world-as-it-could-be. The organ that sees actual situations is the eye, but the organ that 'sees' *potential* situations is the *brain*.

This newfound ability to conceive of potentials altered our relationship to the world in dramatic ways. Our ability to imagine contrary-to-fact situations did not just introduce artefacts that had never been seen before; it also introduced actions that had never been undertaken before. Indeed, we tend to forget that '[e]verything presently known to each, everything rendered predictable, was at one time unknown to all' (Peterson 1999, p. 48). Washing potatoes, for instance, is actually quite an accomplishment (Hirata *et al.* 2008). One cannot know to rub water on a potato simply by looking harder at these two items. The joint perceptual inputs do not necessitate any specific behaviour, any more than staring at a bunch of ingredients automatically tells one which recipe(s) they permit.

Innovation and discovery thus require a special mindset. According to Peterson, '[o]ur imaginative representations actually constitute our initial adaptations' (1999, p. 71). When we confront territory that has never been mapped before, our mapping must relax the descriptive demands of geography (so to speak) and take on the creative demands of artistry. To extract something concrete from the realm of potentiality, one must venture a bold surmise and act on it. If this surmise proves fertile in one's practical dealings, it can be replicated by one's peers, who will thereby take their own imaginations to the next level. Hence, as Peterson rightly observes, '[t]he fact of our sociability [...] increases our chances of exposure to creative intelligence' (1999, p. 75).

What did early humans do once they began to envision different worlds? The first order of business was no doubt to address basic needs — obtaining food, constructing shelter, etc. We modified objects to suit those ends. Eventually, after building tools, we built tools to build tools. In both cases, the starting materials were supplied by the world. However, '[t]he object [...] serves us as a source of limitless possibility' (1999, p. 66). As we became more adept at turning our imagined worlds into reality, we eventually had the freedom to wonder: why can't we create something ourselves, entirely? That is when we invented words.

I can emit a sound resembling a rooster's crow to signify a rooster, but I can also stipulate that the arbitrary sound 'rooster' will stand for that bird — even if all that glues this label is a consistent decision to make it so. Every word we use is thus the product of an arbitrary decision, even if we cannot pinpoint who made that decision or when it was made. Once the decision becomes widely adopted, it settles into place as a large-scale pattern. We might compare this arbitrary assign-ment of meaning to driving on a given side of the road. As the different conventions of the UK and the US show, we are free to pick either side. But if we want to enjoy the benefits of systematic use, we have to stick with the convention we pick. Our established preference for one street side is what evolutionary theorists call a 'frozen accident' (see Crick 1968). Decisions with no causal basis can thus have tangible causal effects when those decisions are sufficiently replicated—just try driving on the wrong side of the road. Similarly, using words any which way means that one will not be understood.

Words may be conventional on the surface, but they are actually conceptual tools that help us group things and events in the world. There is nothing conventional about this. In fact, some of the groupings conveyed by words such as nouns are directly available to our senses. Suppose, for instance, that I must separate a pile of fruits into two baskets labelled 'apples' and 'oranges'. It does not take much abstraction to grasp that apples have important similarities with each other and important differences from oranges. Because the fault line between the groups is easy to grasp, putting the fruits into the distinct baskets will not be very difficult. Often, though, the rationale for categorizing things is not obvious. If an uneducated person came upon a beached whale, for example, she could be forgiven for thinking that it was a large fish and not a mammal.

Once humans were alerted to the fact that the world has a hidden structure, they started mapping that structure and sharing their findings. Our lexicon of words increased and, with it, our understanding. Consider the word 'liar'. What unites all liars? Clearly, our eyes cannot distinguish liars and honest persons in the same way that they distinguish apples and oranges. Picking out the essential features requires more work. Humans are constantly trading and comparing their maps of the world, so it is imperative to know which maps to trust. Once we abstract out what unites all liars, we can craft a definition and encapsulate it with a word. This word can then enter the shared vocabulary of our community. Since it is 'primarily our companions and their actions (or inactions) that stabilize or destabilize our emotions' (Peterson 1999, p. 59), a child who learns to properly apply the word 'liar' acquires a social skill that has tremendous survival value.

The complexity of social facts is staggering. For instance, a layperson will say that so-and-so looked 'sad', but an experienced acting coach will distinguish many species underneath that genus, such as being 'melancholic', being 'dejected', being 'glum', and so on. The availability of these words influences the amount of information we can extract. This holds even at the perceptual level. For instance, if one coins the word 'marown' for the colour between maroon and brown, one can learn to track that specific hue and gradually detect it in one's visual experience. According to Peterson, this 'capacity to create novel [...] categories of interpretation [...] literally allows us to carve the world out of the undifferentiated mass of unobserved and unencountered "existence"' (1999, p. 66).

The human appreciation of language's power seems to go back quite a bit. In his Biblical lectures, Peterson explored the idea that words help us discern patterns amid informational noise. In the Judeo-Christian tradition, 'it is the *Logos* — the word of God — that creates order from chaos' (1999, p. 100). Peterson believes that this 'explicit stress placed by the Judeo-Christian tradition on the primacy of the word and its metaphorical equivalents makes it somewhat unique in the pantheon of creation myths' (1999, p. 111).

Whatever one thinks of Peterson's interpretation, he is surely right that '[t]he *word* enables differentiated thought', which in turn 'heightens the capacity for exploratory maneuvering' (1999, p. 66). When we start using new words like 'whale', 'liar', or the made-up colour 'marown', we open up new possibilities for perception and action. Some situations require coarse-grained distinctions, whereas other situations require fine-grained distinctions. Because the degree of focus has a default resting place (Peterson 1999, p. 96; see Rosch 1978), '[w]ords have a power that belie their ease of use' (Peterson 1999, p. 252). We should not let this ease of use fool us, though. Since words determine what gets noticed or unnoticed, policing words essentially means policing minds. Peterson's observations in philosophy of language thus connect with his views in metaphysics, epistemology, ethics, and politics. Indeed, it could be argued that '[w]hat makes Peterson's approach to free speech stand out is how deep its philosophical roots go down [...]. Free speech is grounded [...] in reality and our relationship with it' (Roberts 2020, p. 59).

As the popular *Harry Potter* novels remind us, one cannot combat an evil that one does not name. Conversely, the right words uttered in the right circumstances can have far-reaching positive effects. That is why Peterson enjoins us to be precise in our speech (2018a, pp. 259–83). As he writes, '[t]he word brings to mind events and actions, sequenced in a particular manner', so '[a]n entire behavioral hierarchy can be undermined by a well-chosen creative phrase [...]' (1999, p. 253).

Here, then, are two words that can literally change the world: *speak up*.

Who should be doing the speaking? The answer is deceptively simple: *me*. It is natural to think that collective problems require collective solutions. However, this way of thinking runs against the hard fact that group agency is not possible. When a group of people act, the actions are performed by the parts, not the whole. To be sure, those parts must coordinate their actions. But, in the end, the whole itself is not a whole but a collection of individuals (Champagne 2014).

The distinction between a whole and a collection is an easy one to miss, so it is understandable that humans first approached social ills with an agent-like view of society. To this day, people often say things like 'Society does such-and-such', 'Society believes that such-and-such', or 'Society needs such-and-such'. Strictly speaking, though, societies cannot do, believe, or need anything. As a result, any plan of action predicated on this misguided ontology cannot succeed. Politicians may like to talk about '*the* German people' or '*the* American people' in the singular. In reality, though, there are German *people* and American *people*, in the plural. This nuance makes all the difference. Focusing on 'society' while neglecting the individual is a bit like trying to purchase a 'dozen' eggs without buying twelve eggs. It cannot be done, so any plan predicated on that idea is doomed to fail.

What distinguishes Peterson's message from that of mainstream pundits is its steadfast advocacy of individual responsibility. If you find the world around you wanting in some way, then you must change how *you* act. It is by changing yourself that you stand a chance of changing the world. If the circumstances are right, one can be raised in a cultural environment that conveys this idea in its myths and narratives. Yet since individualism is not obvious, Peterson presents it as a hardwon result. Every culture has heroes, villains, and allegories to capture the domain of balance between the known and the unknown. Owing to selection pressures, these narrative patterns have survived because they serve fundamental human needs and ends. The main end being sought is arguably the betterment of oneself and the world around one. Narratives orient us toward that goal by giving us concrete examples of how to act and how not to act.

In keeping with Peterson's claim that no map is ever complete, the messages contained in such narratives must be open to continual improvement. Peterson thinks that this is what happened in the transition from the Old Testament to the New Testament. At the risk of oversimplifying, Peterson sees the Old Testament as addressing the salvation of tribes or peoples, whereas the New Testament locates this salvation at the individual scale. The figure of Christ in particular acts as a focal point. Indeed, Peterson draws much inspiration from the image of Jesus bearing the weight of his cross, alone. In

Peterson's interpretation, Christianity enjoins its followers to assume *personal* responsibility for the world's ills. The Bible can thus be seen as an attempt to develop, in a narrative format, a revolutionary political idea: the individual, not the group, is the (only) agent of real change. This idea may now be stated with self-reflective clarity as a full-fledged philosophical -ism — individualism — but it first had to latch onto concrete historical exemplars such as Jesus.

In his clinical practice, Peterson is routinely reminded of our human flaws and shortcomings. Yet, over the water cooler, the same people who are plagued with personal problems muse about enforcing their preferred vision of the world onto others by force of law. As Peterson puts it: 'If you cannot bring peace to your household, how dare you try to rule a city?' (2018a, p. 158). Interviewers who ask Peterson whether the political situation will get better invariably get the same answer: it might. The only claim that Peterson is willing to make in an unqualified way is that if the preconditions for positive change are not present, such change will certainly not come.

Individuals coordinate their actions by sharing what they know. When individual minds are forbidden from openly pointing out errors, there is no possibility of making corrections and adjustments. As the chronicles of Aleksandr Solzhenitsyn (2018) and Viktor Frankl (2006) show, totalitarian regimes thrive in an environment where this communication of truth is prohibited. By controlling the spread of ideas and banning dissent, such regimes try to institutionalize order at the expense of novelty or chaos. The truth, however, is that no single ideology is immune from error. Discovering and communicating errors and mismatches in a map of meaning is not pleasant, but it is vital. The freedom to publicly express dissent is thus crucial to the growth of knowledge and the improvement of one's conditions. This is an idea found in the work of John Stuart Mill (2002), Charles Sanders Peirce (1931–58), Karl Popper (1971), and others. Peterson's contribution is to make the importance of freedom of speech tangible by embedding it in a meaningful worldview and connecting it with current events (in which Peterson is very much a participant).

Truths are not decided by vote. Rather, truths are discovered by individuals who choose to place the relevant evidence above the opinions of others. Sometimes, a truth gets a warm reception. It is often the case, though, that a truth upsets ingrained beliefs and practices. Nevertheless, Peterson stresses that, over the long haul, tracking the truth is the best course of action. A falsehood is an inaccurate map of the world, so no productive outcome can flow from a falsehood (again, in the long run). No single individual can take in all of the world's truths at a glance. The best way to compensate for our fallible limitations, then, is to share what (little) we do know—even if, by definition, confronting new information is a reminder of our own ignorance. Hence, the chief precondition of any betterment project is the freedom to seek and speak the truth.

Importantly, for the ethical and political outlook advocated by Peterson to deliver its full promise, the repudiation of group agency must be accompanied by an equal insistence on coordination devices. Language is the main device that we use to coordinate our individual actions. At the risk of stating a tautology, ideas (good or bad) replicate only by being replicated. When we replicate truths, we pass along our most accurate cartography of the current state of play. Conversely, lying is like giving instructions that will scramble one's teammates and prevent one from winning. So, if nothing else, one should avoid making claims one knows to be false (Peterson 2018a, pp. 203–30). If one cannot further inquiry, one can at least refrain from hindering inquiry.

To make this concrete, consider the truth that microbes exist. Even today, most people do not have the instruments needed to confirm first-hand the existence of these tiny creatures. Despite being invisible, microbes have a tremendous impact on our lives, notably by transmitting infections.

Importantly, Antonie Van Leeuwenhoek discovered this unhappy fact about disease transmission long before Louis Pasteur devised ways of neutralizing these microorganisms. Van Leeuwenhoek nevertheless shared his discovery, even when the only immediate social results at the time were panic, incredulity, and/or worry. Had he kept silent to protect people's feelings, the eventual solution by Pasteur would never have been devised.

One does not have to be a scientist to appreciate how this policy of truth can usher in a better world. Consider a visit to a hospital. Visitors usually encounter a sign at the entrance instructing them to carefully wash their hands before entering. The truth about microbes and their potential harm is not kept secret but made public. This publicity does not ensure that each and every individual will acquaint themselves with the piece of knowledge and do what it recommends. It is clear, though, that if some sort of medical censorship prevented others from learning about the presence of an invisible threat, little could be done to combat it. So while the sign at the hospital entrance contains a truth, this hard-earned result is useless unless it is openly shared. Once it is shared, it allows multiple individuals to adopt a same course of action: washing one's hands. Peterson's philosophy reminds us that if you wash *your* hands, the *whole* hospital will be clean.

Chapter 7

That upon which one is prepared to act

Hours are wasted every day debating futile questions like 'Was x an act of terror?' or 'Do you think y is more libertarian or classical liberal?' or 'Would you describe z as a theist'? According to the theory of meaning called pragmatism, a word's meaning is best accounted by specifying the actions it engenders. The pragmatist thus asks: if we did label x, y, or z that way, what difference would it make? Only by specifying such a real difference can we establish that pursuing these questions is not a waste of time. For instance: 'It is foolish for Catholics and Protestants to fancy themselves in disagreement about the elements of the sacrament, if they agree in regard to all their sensible effects' (Peirce 1931–58, vol. 5, para. 401). Some current divisive rivalries are grounded in nothing more than name-calling (which caters to the worst tribalist remnants in each of us).

Peterson does not mention pragmatism in his two books, but in conversations and interviews he has noticed affinities between his views and that school of thought. Pragmatism defines belief as 'that upon which a man is prepared to act' (see Wernham 1986). So when Peterson (1999) sets out to map the architecture of belief, he essentially sets out to map the ways in which humans are prepared to act.

It makes sense for Peterson to draw on pragmatism, since this was the first philosophical school to take seriously the revolutionary ideas of Charles Darwin. Following Darwin, scientifically minded American philosophers such as Charles Sanders Peirce (1931–58), William James (1977), and John Dewey (1958) considered knowledge as a tool geared primarily towards survival. Minds are not disembodied spirits that exist only to mirror nature (Rorty 1979). Rather, 'mind' is a term for the activity of a brain organ that is there to help us get by—by whatever means we can muster.

The American pragmatists insisted that, were it not for concrete actions, passively witnessing the environment would not accomplish much. We can think of the difference as one of emphasis. When thinking about what it means to think, we can take our main cue from the eyes that *see* or the hands that *do*. While the contemplative view generates a sceptical worry (expressed most memorably by Descartes) that we might be massively deceived by our senses, the pragmatist replies that were such a massive deception the case, we would have gone extinct long ago. The fact that we are still around does not attest to some pre-existing cosmic order, but it is evidence that our collective attempt to form correct beliefs is not hopeless.

Pragmatism views knowing as an activity that unfolds in a sequence of belief, doubt, inquiry, and the restoration of belief. In order to properly understand this account, one has to understand how it involves actions, dispositions, and habits. Let us start with actions.

If you say that you believe *x* but never act in an *x* way, then according to the pragmatist definition of belief you do not really believe *x*. For example, if you claim to be against smoking but in fact smoke two packs of cigarettes per day, your deeds are the indicator of what you really believe. Conversely, I believe that the chair underneath me will hold my weight, because I am prepared to sit on it without hesitation. Beliefs are not verbal statements or mental pictures that only the believer has access to, by introspection. On the contrary, beliefs are rendered visible by the public occurrences that they engender. So when one's verbal pronouncements or introspections are at odds with one's tangible actions, the actions always win. To hold otherwise would be to turn speech and reflection into magical tools. I might say with great confidence that I am a bus driver. But if I have never driven a bus and never will, then I am simply not what I claim to be. Passing a lie detector test does not bypass the fact that actions speak louder than words.

It is easy to see why Peterson describes himself as a pragmatist. According to him, '[t]he mythic universe is *a place to act*, not *a place to perceive*' (1999, p. 9). Peterson also shares pragmatism's hard-nosed acceptance that '[t]here appears to exist some "natural" or [...] "absolute" constraints on the manner in which human beings may act as individuals and in society. Some moral presuppositions and theories are *wrong*; human nature is not infinitely malleable' (1999, p. 11; for a kindred view, see Champagne 2015b).

Pragmatism sees the success of an action as the most potent proof that the action in question got something right about the world. We may not understand which parts of a belief were right. I may correctly believe, for instance, that a given smoothie improves my health, without being able to identify which ingredient(s) is/are responsible for this success. Similarly, in his study of myth, Peterson shows how humanity's most basic narratives and archetypes served us well, even if we cannot quite pinpoint how and why they have benefitted us over time. Their instrumental utility speaks in their favour. By the same rationale, a belief that would be completely wrong yet lead to good results would make no sense. When a bridge collapses, the world informs us that the beliefs of the architect and/or engineers must have been wrong *somewhere*.

When pragmatists define belief as 'that upon which a man *is prepared* to act', they do not require the action(s) at hand to be performed here and now. Rather, to be credited with a belief, it is enough that one stands ready to act in a certain way. In philosophical parlance, pragmatists construe beliefs as 'dispositions' to act (Engel 2005). This nuance is important, otherwise an exclusive focus on present action would lead to attributing far fewer beliefs than one in fact possesses. For instance, I surely have a belief about how I should conduct myself at a funeral, but since I am at my desk right now, this belief will manifest itself only if and when I find myself in the appropriate circumstance. Even so, my body currently houses this readiness to act, in the same way that a ball placed atop a hill stores potential kinetic energy (that will be released as kinetic energy on the day it rolls downhill).

Humans, however, are not balls. Whereas balls are pushed, humans are pulled, since they move in a way that exhibits purpose. Of course, as chunks of matter, humans can be pushed too—when a prison guard forces an inmate into a prison cell, she effectively treats the inmate like a ball. Still, the usual (and preferable) way for humans to move is deliberately, by following a goal. I might, for instance, enter my bedroom looking forward to quietly reading a book in bed. My belief that the book awaits me by my bedside may have a distinctive feel (Champagne 2018a). Even so, that belief is not just a feeling; it is something I am prepared to act upon.

Since most worthwhile activities (like reading a book, going to work, sustaining a marriage, etc.) require repeated actions, most of our beliefs are things we are prepared to *habitually* act upon. Such habituation is important, because it diminishes the demands on our cognitive systems, in so far as '[t]o know something is to do it automatically, without thinking, to categorize it at a glance (or less than a glance), or to ignore it entirely' (Peterson 1999, p. 150). Habits that still work place us in what Peterson calls 'order', whereas habits that are no longer up to the task of rendering our experience predictable place us in what Peterson calls 'chaos'. Like Peterson, pragmatists make it clear that we revise our beliefs only when they break down. No belief, no matter how well established, is immune from this possibility of eventual failure. 'This is because chaos and order are interchangeable, as well as eternally juxtaposed. There is nothing so certain that it cannot vary' (Peterson 2018a, p. 12). Pragmatism is an account of how we cope with this.

The sequence of habit, breakdown of habit, and restoration of habit is how beliefs get hammered into conformity with the world. We must strive to overcome our ignorance, so '[t]his process of necessary eternal overcoming constantly constructs and transforms our behavioral repertoires and representational schemas' (Peterson 1999, p. 150). Peterson's pragmatism-friendly contribution consists in showing how humans pass on their most successful coping strategies in a narrative format. The story of all stories is about how surprise gets transformed into habit. Since '[t]hings that are bitter, feared and avoided must be approached and conquered' for life to be worthwhile, the mythical tales that have withstood the test of time are about 'the admirable individual, engaged in voluntary, creative, communicative endeavor; they portray that individual generating a personality capable of withstanding the fragility of being' (Peterson 2004, p. 10).

To be more than a one-off fluke, such antifragility requires repeated exposure to adversity. William James, who was both a pragmatist and a pioneer in psychology, held that

> we are subject to the law of habit in consequence of the fact that we have bodies. The plasticity of the living matter of our nervous system, in short, is the reason why we do a thing with difficulty the first time, but soon do it more and more easily, and finally, with sufficient practice, do it semi-mechanically, or with hardly any consciousness at all. Our nervous systems have [...] *grown* to the way in which they

have been exercised, just as a sheet of paper or a coat, once creased or folded, tends to fall forever afterward into the same identical folds. (James 1916, p. 65)

Beliefs are not New Age psychic states that escape scientific detection, but rather more or less stable patterns of action that can be observed and objectively studied. Trying to study meaning without attending to practical actions would thus be pointless since, as Peterson says, '[m]eaning means implication for behavioral output' (1999, p. 13). It may be that when one acts in a habitual manner, one consults some sort of mental picture to guide one's actions. I might, for instance, have some (rudimentary or well-defined) image of my ideal self in mind when I dress professionally and go to work every day. I have crafted this self-image over time, by collecting real and fictional exemplars from my surrounding culture. According to Peterson, '[i]t is our mythological conventions, operating implicitly or explicitly, that guide our choices' (1999, p. 10). However, what matters is not my private contemplation of such images but rather the various actions they lead to. Far from being private, those actions can be witnessed (and thus assessed) by other people, such as relatives, colleagues, and bosses.

Peirce, arguably the foremost American pragmatist, regarded pragmatism as 'an application of the sole principle of logic which was recommended by Jesus; "Ye may know them by their fruits"' (1931–58, vol. 5, para. 402, fn. 2). Of course, in contrast with religion, pragmatism shuns all dogmas and demands that one always stand ready to revise or abandon a belief. Peirce held that 'the scientific spirit requires a man to be at all times ready to dump his whole cart-load of beliefs, the moment experience is against them' (1931–58, vol. 1, para. 55). Since we are not likely to see revised and updated versions of the Bible, it is doubtful that religious conviction and pragmatism are compatible. Taken in isolation, the recommendation to judge a tree by its yield is spot on. Still, in the final analysis, religious conviction is inimical to open inquiry. We can err and/or say stupid things, but there are no analogues of 'sacrilege' and 'blasphemy' in secular discourse.

I will revisit these themes in the second part of this book. For now, let us note that Peterson deems it important—indeed vital—for an individual and a society to acknowledge fallibility and develop channels for dealing with the unknown. It seems sensible, then, to endorse what Peirce saw as the First Rule of Reason:

> Upon this first, and in one sense this sole, rule of reason, that in order to learn you must desire to learn, and in so desiring not be satisfied with what you already incline to think, there follows one corollary which itself deserves to be inscribed upon every wall of the city of philosophy: Do not block the way of inquiry. (Peirce 1931–58, vol. 1, para. 135)

The sooner we drag some unknown x into the territory of the known, the sooner we can assess that x and respond to it accordingly. Hence, dogmatic belief is not just the enemy of science, it is the enemy of the heroic within each of us—of the struggle to look for better beliefs and improve.

The practical consequences of the beliefs we adopt are sometimes revealed in a dramatic moment, like a bridge collapse. Most of the time, the merit of our beliefs is revealed in the long run. A saying (by Ralph Waldo Emerson or John W. Beckwaith?) captures well how dispositions, actions, and habits link together: 'Sow a thought and you reap an action; sow an act and you reap a habit; sow a habit and you reap a character; sow a character and you reap a destiny'. Since ideas have the potential to grow, Peterson sows a series of deceptively simple thoughts: 'Quit drooping and hunching around. Speak your mind. Put your desires forward, as if you had a right to them—at least the same right as others. Walk tall and gaze forthrightly ahead' (Peterson 2018a, pp. 27–28). If you put this nice-sounding advice into action, it becomes more than just nice-sounding advice.

Personal transformation requires real action; thinking harder will not do it. But if you act habitually in the right manner, your actions will be more than reliable indicators of your character; they will *be* your character. Since a society is comprised of individuals who are in turn comprised of their actions, Peterson holds that reforms to society must be rooted in tangible changes in one's individual actions.

As the very existence of this book attests, exchanging ideas via language is important. But such a linguistic exchange should never eclipse the fact that the world is changed by doing better things, not by talking more. Fans with a surface sympathy for Peterson's ideas may log on to Twitter or Reddit to make short or rambling posts about the virtue of justice or the evils of totalitarian mindsets. However, someone who truly believes in Peterson's ideas routinely puts those ideas into practice in his or her daily affairs. Given the human propensity for imitation, these actions turn each person into a walking advertisement for their beliefs. Still, the take-away lesson of pragmatism is that it does not matter whether one's deeds go unnoticed. The causal efficacy of an act resides in its practical effects, not in the thumbs-up 'likes' it accumulates.

The reason that moralizing on social media is so prevalent is simple. When one expresses indignation at the latest (real or invented) transgression, there are two possible outcomes: one's expression of indignation will be either overlooked or picked up. If it is picked up, then one has a chance of attaining internet nirvana by attracting 'followers' and 'going viral'. But if one's rant is overlooked, one loses absolutely nothing. Compare, for example, what would happen if lottery tickets were offered to the public for free. Given the prospect of winning millions of dollars, it would make perfect sense for everyone to obtain lots of tickets, every time. You have nothing to lose.

As a result of this toxic system of incentives, '[a]t no point in history have so many non-risk-takers, that is, those with no personal exposure, exerted so much control' (Taleb 2014, p. 6). Merely by logging on, anonymous mobs can destroy anyone at any time — without incurring any damage whatsoever. Character assassinations are routinely attempted on Peterson. However, by standing his ground and fine-tuning his message in response to criticisms, Peterson (mostly) practices the anti-fragility that he preaches.

Make no mistake: he preaches too. Indeed, the journalist Wendy Mesley once asked Peterson whether he is more like the American television preacher Billy Graham or the Canadian communication theorist Marshall McLuhan. Peterson answered that he is like 'Billy McLuhan'. This is a clever reply. However, while Marshall McLuhan is required reading on university campuses, Billy Graham is not. Since the term 'preaching' carries negative connotations (in academic circles, at least), it would be more charitable to say that Peterson endorses, not just pragmatism, but 'pragmatism as a way of life', to use Ruth Anna Putnam's apt expression. To appreciate this, compare Peterson's views with Putnam's take on William James's philosophy:

> James emphasizes not only that the moral life requires 'pluck and will, dogged endurance and insensibility to danger', but also that this 'strenuous mood' can be sustained only if one believes 'that acts are really good and bad', and that involves, for him, both a belief in indeterminism and in the objectivity of moral values. Morality, objective values, and with them obligations exist whenever there are persons who care for one another. 'One rock with two loving souls upon it... would have as thoroughly moral a constitution as any possible world.... There would be real good things and real bad things... obligations, claims and expectations; obediences, refusals, and

disappointments... a moral life, whose active energy would have no limit but the intensity of interest in each other'. Objectivity in ethics depends, then, on the possibility of resolving conflicts, of arriving at shared values, of jointly espousing more inclusive ideals. That possibility rests on the fact that we have sympathetic as well as egoistic instincts, which 'arise, so far as we can tell, on the same psychological level'. However, for James, objectivity is more than mere intersubjectivity. His insistence on the imperfections of the world and on the possibility of moral progress suggests that there is a standard outside not only this or that thinker but outside any particular collection of them, just as scientific truth is not determined by the opinions of any particular collection of scientists. 'There can be no final truth in ethics any more than in physics until the last man has had his experience and said his say'. In ethics, though not in physics, this notion of a final truth seems to be clearly distinguishable from belief in a divine thinker. For, though James says that 'ethics have as genuine and real a foothold in a universe where the highest consciousness is human, as in a universe where there is a God as well', he also asserts that 'in a merely human world without a God, the appeal to our moral energy falls short of its maximal stimulating power. Life, to be sure, is even in such a world a genuinely ethical symphony; but it is played in the compass of a couple of poor octaves, and the infinite scale of values fails to open up'. I want to put this aside. (Putnam and Putnam 2017, pp. 361–62)

Everything in this brilliant gloss sounds Petersonian—minus the final point about God, which Peterson does not put aside.

Chapter 8

Gods, utopias, and other unreachable ideals we project

Peterson spends quite a bit of time talking about religion, so it is normal to wonder what his religious views are, exactly. A straightforward answer is hard to come by. When asked whether he believes in God, Peterson typically answers, 'I act as if God exists'. The 'as if' portion strikes both theists and atheists as a dodge (Johnson 2018). There is ample merit to that complaint. However, the fact that Peterson brings up his own actions when formulating an answer about God's existence speaks to his pragmatist orientation.

To say that something exists is equivalent to saying that one stands ready to behave in various ways. Hence, '[a] car, as we perceive it, is not a thing, or an object. It is instead something that takes us somewhere we want to go' (Peterson 2018a, p. 265). Similarly, my belief in my refrigerator is nothing more than a disposition to put eggs in that cold box when I return from the grocery store, ask friends for help when I need to move it to another house, and so on. When we focus on such actions, as pragmatism recommends that we do, we make a topic tractable. So, like any belief, verbally proclaiming belief in God means very little if one cannot specify the way(s) in which this belief makes one act differently.

As we have now seen, Peterson calls on the achievements of science, notably evolutionary biology, when formulating his arguments. Peterson is aware that '[a] succession of great scientists and iconoclasts has demonstrated that [...] there is no God in heaven' (1999, p. 5). But according to him, '[i]t is reason's remarkable ability, and its own recognition of that ability that leads it to believe it possesses absolute knowledge and can therefore replace, or do without, God' (1999, p. 314). Interestingly, despite undermining belief in God, Charles Darwin is never mentioned by Peterson in this regard. In any event, Peterson's work on myths and dreams makes him sensitive to the possibility that not everything can be caught in the net of scientific explanation. This seems to imply that when it comes to the question of God's existence, the most that scientific reason can recommend is agnosticism.

According to Peterson, scientists and thinkers who deny the existence of God suffer from a kind of intellectual hubris. This 'presumption of absolute knowledge, which is the cardinal sin of the rational spirit, [...] is ineradicably opposed to the "humility" of creative exploration', which Peterson sees as 'the necessary precondition for confrontation with the unknown' (1999, p. 316). In a way, this statement is puzzling. After all, most scientists are fallibilists about their own field's accomplishments. Few physicists will say, for example, that the latest cutting-edge theory gets the world perfectly right, since to do so would be to ignore the history of science, littered as it is with disproven theories. Peterson suggests that such fallibilism should hold across the board—especially when dealing with topics that are, by definition, out of reach. We should approach these mysteries with a sense of awe (see Keltner and Jonathan Haidt 2003).

Despite all this, Peterson accepts that '[t]he "death of God" in the modern world looks like an accomplished fact' (1999, p. 245). He nevertheless thinks that something important has been lost along the way. In his view, the 'existential upheaval and philosophical uncertainty characteristic of the first three-quarters of the twentieth century demonstrate that we have not yet settled back on firm ground' (1999, p. 245). We have managed to survive two world wars, but '[o]ur current miraculous state of relative peace and economic tranquility should not blind us to the fact that gaping holes remain in our spirits' (1999, p. 245).

In an attempt to fill this spiritual gap, Peterson considers in a more charitable light what humans believed *before* they abandoned religious belief. As he says, '[t]he cosmos described by mythology was *not* the same place known to the practitioners of modern science — but that does not mean it was not *real*' (1999, p. 8). Clearly, most myths are false. However, the point of most mythological narratives, Peterson argues, is not to describe the world but rather to explain how one might *act* in the world. Stories, on this view, tell us how to structure our lives. In order to orient themselves in their social and natural environments, humans need to envision a worst-case scenario (to be avoided) and a best-case scenario (to be sought). 'We have not yet found God above, nor the Devil below, because we do not yet understand where "above" and "below" might be found' (Peterson 1999, p. 8). Those who think that God sits on a cloud thus miss the point.

According to Peterson, to jettison God is to jettison the idea of a supreme ideal. Conceptions of this ideal have evolved over time, so the notion of God as we know it today is the culmination of millennia of hard work. Polytheism, on this account, is a rough draft that must eventually be superseded. This allows Peterson to interpret the historical record as a progression. According to his interpretation, 'in the earliest stages of representation, deities are viewed as pluralistic, and as individualistic and fractious members of a supracelestial (that is, transpersonal and immortal) community' (1999, p. 134). An experience such as jealousy, for example, feels more like the effect of an outside agency than some internal psychological mechanism. Persons are the agents that we understand best, so it is tempting to view this emotion as 'caused' by a person-like god, in this case 'the god of jealousy'. The full range of human experience can be carved this way.

If every god reigns over a qualitatively distinct experiential domain—the god of love governs love, the god of war governs war, and so on—what possible utility might there be in positing a single, overarching God? The thing that all experiences share is that they are experiences. When we reach this abstraction, we reach the highest abstraction possible.

Good events and bad events presuppose a consciousness that partakes in those events. 'This idea was developed (abstracted and generalized) further by the Greeks, who attributed to each male Greek a soul, and taken to its logical conclusion by the Jews and the Christians, who granted every person absolute and inviolable individual worth before (or [potential] identity with) God' (Peterson 1999, p. 185). The God of monotheism was thus arrived at 'as a consequence of combat' among the various gods of the old polytheistic regimes (1999, p. 193). 'Later, [these gods] are integrated into a hierarchy, as the culture becomes more integrated, more sure about relative valuation and moral virtue—and a single god, with a multitude of related features, comes to dominate' (1999, p. 134).

This collective reflection on divinity and the human condition is hard for scholars to discern, Peterson contends, because it is 'a process extending over untold centuries' (1999, p. 192). Tracing the history of this process requires that one engage in 'an abstracted and poetic description of the manner in which emergent behavioral patterns and interpretive schemas—moral positions, so to speak—fight for predominance, and therefore organize themselves, over the course of time' (1999, p. 193). Peterson's advocacy of a free market of ideas connects with his claim that '[t]he many gods of archaic conceptualization became the single ruler of more modern

religious thinking as a consequence of spiritual competition—
so to speak' (1999, p. 314). So whereas most historians credit
Darwin with dealing the death blow to monotheistic worldviews, Peterson thinks that Darwinian theory can explain how
the monotheistic conception of God gradually came into
existence.

If it makes sense to say that particular lives unfold on a
canvas of life, then humans seem to need some way to con-
ceptualize this abstraction. Thus, the God of monotheism
'places himself outside of or beyond worldly change, and
unites the temporal opposites within the great circle of his
being' (Peterson 1999, p. 144).

So what does it mean to 'act as if God exists'? Peterson does
not say, but here is one charitable gloss. When I evaluate my
options and perform an act that I regard as best, it seems that I
logically commit myself not just to this act, but also to the idea
that this would again be the best course of action if the same
circumstances were to present themselves again. If, for
instance, I come to the conclusion that putting on my seatbelt
before driving to work is a good thing to do *this morning*, then
in principle it is a good thing to do *every* morning. Actions are
thus subject to a form of reasoning by analogy, such that
mastering a prescription like 'I should put my seatbelt on'
ostensibly requires understanding that, all other things being
equal, 'I should *always* put my seatbelt on'. Same contextual
input, same behavioural output—to the extent, that is, that
one's actions are principled.

Reasoning by analogy carries conclusions over to anything
that is deemed similar. My future self is similar to me, but so
are other people. Hence, if putting on my seatbelt is good for
me, then it does not take much to conclude that this action is
good for *anybody* who would be in a situation like mine.
Because the vague placeholder 'anybody' fits everybody,
particular assessments are always a few reasoning steps away
from being given a worldwide range. What starts out as a

personal reflection on how to act can thus transform into a prescription applying to all people.

Historically, this ability to 'universalize' prescriptions has received grandiose interpretations. Plato thought it gave us insight into a supernatural world uncorrupted by the imperfections of everyday life. Christianity absorbed this genial metaphysical outlook. Inheriting this lineage, Immanuel Kant held that any action that cannot be universalized cannot be regarded as moral. Indeed, Kant held that you should '[a]ct only according to that maxim whereby you can at the same time will that it should become a universal law' (1993, p. 30). There are, however, more modest ways of looking at universalization. Instead of seeing it as the trace of another world or as the litmus test of morality, we can see universalization as a straightforward consequence of our ability to draw analogies. Peterson's work can shed light on this ability.

One of the main tenets of Peterson's account is that humans act out their beliefs long before they learn to say why they hold those beliefs. Since the first phase of our life is marked by an inability to use language, our main way of acquiring new patterns of behaviour is by observation. The patterns of behaviour that we see around us are essentially narratively structured. Some of these stories are planned and fictional. However, the drama of daily life offers us a steady supply of real heroes and villains. As Peterson writes, '[w]e learn the story, *which we do not understand* (which is to say, cannot make explicit), by watching' (1999, p. 75). As a result, '[w]e observe others acting in a manner we find admirable, and duplicate their actions' (1999, p. 75). These imitation-worthy actions constitute our earliest moral guidance.

Peterson draws on his account of goal directedness to explain how certain actions spread among individuals. Suppose that I want to obtain an apple on a tree branch but cannot reach it. Suddenly, a member of my species comes along, shakes the tree, and obtains the apple. In a flash, I acquire a pattern of action that, given my intended aim (of eating the apple), has a positive value. This account is attractive because '[n]o independent "instinct" necessarily needs to be postulated [...] all that may be necessary is the capacity to observe that another has obtained a goal that is also valued by the observer (that observation provides the necessary motivation), and the skill to duplicate the procedures observed to lead to such fulfillment' (Peterson 1999, p. 76). People who achieve the ends that we seek thus enjoy a special status. 'The worshipful attitude that small boys adopt towards their heroes, for example, constitutes the outward expression of the force that propels them towards embodying, or incarnating (or even inventing) oft ill-defined heroic qualities themselves' (Peterson 1999, p. 76). Although parents or guardians are not superheroes, they have a tremendous responsibility to serve as good role models, because a child's natural penchant for imitation is on twenty-four hours a day, not just when a parent wishes it.

Peterson's account sheds light on our ability to universalize moral assessments, because '[m]imetic propensity, expressed in imitative action [...] allows the *ability* of each to become the *capability* of all' (1999, p. 76). Owing to reasoning by analogy, which is a very basic form of inference, actions deemed appropriate for one person are deemed appropriate for all persons. However, one of the virtues of Peterson's account, in my estimation, is that it explains this tendency to universalize while at the same time enjoining us to halt universalization, by focusing on *action* instead of *activism*.

Reasoning by analogy is rampant in ethics because it conveniently shifts the focus from oneself to others. With our gaze fixated on the supposedly universal application of a given course of action, we easily forget that we alone have the agency needed to bring that course of action down to earth. Peterson thus rightly praises Aleksandr Solzhenitsyn, who 'instead of cursing fate, shook the whole pathological system of communist tyranny to its core' by taking personal responsibility for that tyranny (Peterson 2018a, p. 155).

Talk of responsibilities in the abstract, which is a defining feature of deontological ethics, pales in comparison to asking oneself: 'Are you truly shouldering your responsibilities?' (Peterson 2018a, p. 157). If you play soccer and you want your team to win, you do so not by controlling the minds of others, but by moving your two legs, keeping your eyes open for a pass, looking for well-positioned teammates to pass to, aiming well if you take a shot, and so on. We often must coordinate what we do, but ultimately, individual action is the only action there is. Sustained personal responsibility is incredibly taxing. Verbal complaints, by contrast, exert no cost and achieve very little. More problematically, such complaints can be aimed in all directions. The person you think is immoral likely thinks that *you* are immoral—and she may think this with more vigour and conviction than you. When the only thing people share is their nostril flare, talking at cross purposes will not yield anything productive. Meanwhile, there is a pile of better things to do. So as Peterson says: 'Set your house in perfect order before you criticize the world' (2018a, p. 159).

Chances are that if you manage to bring your own actions into conformity with what you think is right, you will emerge from your house only to realize that the world around you no longer needs any radical interference. This is because universalization is operative in the world—it just doesn't work the way that most philosophers and theologians think. To be a realist (about objective values or God or whatever) is just to recognize that the thing believed in does not need to be believed in order to exist (Champagne 2016b).

The natural penchant for imitation ensures that when you do something you deem right, you radiate the non-verbal sign 'Do like me'. Peterson's work shows why it is important to keep this particular sign non-verbal. As one student put it: 'Don't just criticize woke culture—constitute something that will take its place' (Handa 2019). You can, if you wish, spoil such constructive work and leadership-by-example by proselytizing. Such a verbal display, though, will not magically persuade others to adopt your beliefs. Rather, it will simply redirect your finite resources away from the individual actions that alone give your beliefs a causal foothold in the world.

Chapter 9

Hierarchies, good and bad

Peterson gestures a lot when he speaks. His most frequent gesture is using his hands to draw the shape of a triangle in the air. Peterson invokes this pyramidal shape whenever he discusses hierarchies. Hierarchical structures are key to understanding his philosophical outlook, but the negative connotations attached to the word 'hierarchy' have obscured the important point(s) that Peterson is trying to make.

Usually, when people think of hierarchies, they think of a caste system, where each person is assigned to an arbitrary social rank that cannot be overcome. Hierarchies, on this view, are one of the main sources of oppression. Hence, if oppression must be fought, so must hierarchies. Peterson, however, has something very different in mind when he discusses hierarchies. According to him, they are basic structures that arise whenever something is sought but is limited in quantity/availability. Hierarchies, on this view, can actually be a good thing.

We only have so much time in any given day to carry out our projects. Like it or not, this limitation forces us to prioritize what we do. I might, for instance, spend two hours watching a movie, but if I spend my time this way, then I cannot use those two hours for something else, such as reading a book. Now a typical day might allow me to squeeze in both of those activities. However, at some point, something must be left out. The problem of deciding what falls below that cut-off point is what compels us to rank our values from most important to least important. Determining such a ranking is not always obvious. Still, were one to know with full clarity the maximal fit between one's values and the world, the resulting structure would be hierarchical (see Champagne 2011a).

This hierarchical pattern occurs not only at the individual scale, but also socially. Consider dentists. Clearly, the number of dentists that an economy can support is indexed to the number of mouths in that economy. Other factors come into play; if people really value dental health, for example, a given population will allow more dentists to make a living. It is clear, though, that the principles of supply and demand impose a cap on how many people can successfully work as dentists. There can't be a society where the main wealth-production engine is the fact that we all clean each other's teeth. How, then, do we determine the cut-off point that lets some people practice that profession? Peterson argues that, ideally, this should be determined by a contest of competence. Like any complex skill, mastery of dentistry comes in degrees. We award degrees in all fields of study precisely to signal in an open (and hopefully consistent) way that a minimum level of competence has been met. Yet as any patient can attest, even when they hold a licence, some dentists are better than others. Recognized certification combined with one's ability to attract and retain clients will mean that only competent dentists get to practice their trade. Once again, translating this into a ranking is not always obvious. Still, it is clear that were one to rank dentists from most liked to least liked, the resulting structure would be hierarchical.

A hierarchy, according to Peterson, is a map that tells one what to prefer. If A is above B in a hierarchy, and limitations (in time, money, or whatever else) force you to choose, then you should choose A. Although we rarely think of romantic matters in such stark logical terms, the selection of a mate also follows these general principles. Again, the possibility of placing potential partners in a hierarchy does not mean that one in fact has a meticulous rank or that one gets to be with whomever one wants most. Still, it would be weird if one were to pick the person that one deems least suited to be one's partner. It seems, then, that humans (and all animals generally) have recourse to some rudimentary map that tells them whom to prefer.

Unfortunately, some people are so put off by the word 'hierarchy' that they are not receptive to these important points. Peterson is partly to blame. Not only does he pick a counter-productive label, he sometimes equivocates in the use of that label. On the one hand, we can be concerned with a *value* hierarchy — 'an edifice of meaning, which contains within it hierarchical organization of experiential valence' (Peterson 1999, p. 13). On the other hand, we can be concerned with a *dominance* hierarchy — 'a social arrangement which determines access to desired commodities' (1999, p. 267). Peterson often wobbles between these two different concepts.

Consider, for example, this seemingly innocuous passage: 'You work in an office; you are climbing the corporate ladder. Your daily activity reflects this superordinate goal' (Peterson 1999, p. 23). These two statements gloss over an important nuance. The corporate ladder is a hierarchical structure that is *socially imposed*. You have no say about who is 'over' you in a workplace. By contrast, the hierarchical ordering of one's daily activities is *individually adopted*. As a result, you can find your-self somewhere 'on' a corporate ladder without any desire to 'climb' that ladder. The hierarchies that others impose on you can therefore differ from the hierarchies that you adopt. I wish Peterson were clearer on this point.

The distinction at hand is crucial. Indeed, politics emerges as a phenomenon precisely because what the individual values is not necessarily what the group (on average) values. Inter-estingly, in a manuscript draft of *Maps of Meaning* dated May

2002 that Peterson has made available online, he originally wrote that '[p]lans (and ends) are granted comparative import-ance [...] in a structure that [...] is very much *like* a dominance hierarchy' (p. 76; my emphasis). However, this important qualification is missing from the final published version (Peterson 1999, p. 84).

Given that Peterson's chosen terminology invites confusion and runs counter to his aims, it might have been wise to adopt a more apt expression that Peterson (1999, p. 479, n. 187) flags, namely 'goal hierarchy' (see Carver and Scheier 1982, p. 113). Of course, the goals of an employee and the goals of an employer could (and ideally should) align. Peterson often says that the best aim would be one deemed good at multiple levels. Yet such maximal fit with individual, familial, and societal scales cannot be a sufficient criterion. Surely one must also experience some pre-reflective pull in the given direction, otherwise making a purely descriptive case that one is good at cooking (say) and that cooks are needed would be enough to show that one *should* be a cook. This would go against Peterson's insistence that 'it is not possible to derive an *ought* from an *is* (this is the "naturalistic fallacy" of David Hume)' (1999, p. 34, see Hume 1960, pp. 469–70). To the extent that this concern has a basis, no amount of facts about one's proclivities and context can amount to a decision. An additional element of voluntarism thus seems required.

Overall, it is not helpful to make an analogy between chosen values and the pecking orders found in animal communities. Most people object to the latter kind of hierarchy, but since values must be organized hierarchically—which is Peterson's real message—the baby gets thrown out with the bath water.

Peterson claims that hierarchical social structures go back as far as lobsters. Lobsters have been around far longer than we have. Yet, like us, these animals organize themselves into well-defined hierarchies. Such hierarchies are established by a series of confrontations aimed at settling who can defeat whom. Since it would be self-defeating, from an evolutionary standpoint, for each member to engage in mortal combat, most of the conflict resolution is acted out in ritual only. 'Sometimes one lobster can tell immediately from the display of claw size that it is much smaller than its opponent, and will back down without a fight' (Peterson 2018a, pp. 5–6). On other occasions, when two lobsters are evenly matched, there will be a show of 'antennae whipping madly and claws folded downward' until 'the more nervous of the lobsters may feel that continuing is not in his best interest' (2018a, p. 6). Only a small portion of these pair-wise assessments of dominance ever escalate to genuine physical fights. When these fights happen, the goal is to flip one's rival on its back. For the most part, though, the con-frontations non-violently resolve who *could* defeat whom, not who *does* defeat whom.

Peterson draws two main lessons from his (no doubt limited) understanding of lobster behaviour. First, he sees it as evidence that humans are not the sole creators of social hierarchies. Hierarchies result from an unequal distribution of whatever a species deems valuable. In the case of lobsters, for example, females prefer successful males, who thus get to select from a larger pool of mating partners. In addition, '[t]he domi-nant male [...] gets the prime real estate and easiest access to the best hunting grounds' (Peterson 2018a, p. 11). Naturally, a lobster that is well fed and sexually satisfied is better equipped to overcome future rivals. Because possessing key resources makes it easier to acquire still more resources, 'it is expo-nentially more worthwhile to be successful' (Peterson 2018a, p. 11).

Sometimes, having x facilitates having still more x, while not having x makes it harder to get x. This results in what is called Pareto distribution (named after the scientist Vilfredo Pareto). The general pattern can be seen in many spheres of activity. As Peterson (2018a, p. 9) points out, unequal distributions that tend toward further inequality explain not just lobster behaviours, but also the population of cities (which attract more people the larger they get) and the growth of stars (which attract more matter the larger they get). It is false, then, to assume that humans are the ones who, because of some inherent flaw or immorality, introduce inequality to what would otherwise be an egalitarian natural paradise. Inequality cannot be the product of, say, capitalism or 'the patriarchy', Peterson argues, because inequality predates the appearance of humans by millions of years.

The case of lobsters inspires Peterson not just on a social scale, but on a psychological scale as well. He is particularly impressed by the fact that '[i]n the aftermath of a losing battle […] [a] vanquished competitor loses confidence, sometimes for days' (2018a, p. 6). The behaviour and brain chemistry of a defeated lobster have many markers of depression. However, it turns out that '[w]hen a lobster that has just lost a battle is exposed to serotonin, it will stretch itself out, advance even on former victors, and fight longer and harder' (2018a, p. 7). In Peterson's view, this is compelling evidence for 'the evolutionary continuity of life on Earth' (2018a, p. 7). In keeping with this evolutionary continuity, Peterson suggests that '[t]here is an unspeakably primordial calculator, deep within you, at the very foundation of your brain, far below your thoughts and feelings', that 'monitors exactly where you are positioned in society' (2018a, p. 15). Human body language and serotonin levels operate in a manner similar to lobsters', so '[i]f you present yourself as defeated, then people will react to you as if you are losing' (Peterson 2018a, p. 26). Conversely, if you consciously take charge of this process and 'start to straighten up, then people will look at and treat you differently' (2018a, p. 26), thereby giving you renewed opportunities to reinvent yourself and improve your social standing.

The two insights, social and psychological, that Peterson gleans from lobster hierarchies are not unrelated. Indeed,

Peterson argues that turning one's life around at the psychological level requires letting go of the worldview that defines all social inequalities as unjust. Peterson says that '[a]nyone with any sense knows that hierarchical structures tilt toward tyranny, and that we have to be constantly wakeful to ensure that all they are isn't just power and tyranny. [...] But that doesn't mean the imperfect hierarchies that we have constructed in our relatively free countries don't at least tilt somewhat toward competence and ability [...]' (Peterson, in Dyson *et al.* 2018, p. 99). One can, if one wishes, view everything as a conflict between oppressor and oppressed. However, Peterson argues that '[i]n societies that are well-functioning [...] *competence*, not power, is a prime determiner of status' (2018a, p. 313). As he puts it: 'No one [...] is equity-minded enough to refuse the service of the surgeon with the best education, the best reputation and, perhaps, the highest earnings' (2018a, p. 313). Peterson's political ideal is not a society where inequalities are eradicated — there are good metaphysical reasons to think that such a levelling can never be carried out — but rather a society where inequalities reflect objective differences in merit and work ethic.

Someone who is currently located on the less desirable end of a Pareto distribution can, with time and effort, improve their lot. It is by no means easy. Orchestrating a reversal of fortunes requires formulating and adhering to a systematic game plan tailored to one's specific context. There is no one-size-fits-all formula for success. Still, according to Peterson, it all begins with a decision to embrace self-affirmation. Even when nothing outside us looks like it is working in our favour, we can at least adopt the posture of a hero. Like making one's bed or eating a balanced breakfast, this seemingly minor act of embodied self-affirmation can have a cascading effect that positively affects our mood and environment. But, for this to happen, one must take control. You control your own spine — you can't plausibly blame 'the system' for refusing to straighten *that*. Thus, as quirky as it may seem, Peterson enjoins us to find inspiration in 'the victorious lobster, with its 350 million years of practical wisdom' (2018a, p. 28).

Peterson insists, however, that humans come hardwired not just with a potential hero within, but with a potential villain there too. In psychology, Sigmund Freud introduced the idea (originally formulated by Arthur Schopenhauer) that our minds include an unconscious portion animated by powerful sexual drives. Freud's student, Carl Jung, suggested that this unconscious also includes dark impulses, such as envy, destruction, and sheer hatred. Peterson takes Jung's troubling suggestion seriously. Using Jung's idea that we each have a 'shadow', Peterson tries to disabuse us of an attractive but severely limited picture. In this picture, there are evil people out there and the moral thing to do is to fight them. As Peterson points out, this picture is attractive because it situates the blame squarely outside us. People who embrace this picture are called upon to act (and perhaps denounce others), but not to change. This widespread picture is thus limited because it completely overlooks the fact that the only domain over which we have control is ourselves. Peterson's message is that, ulti-mately, to change the world, you have to change yourself and fight the evil within you.

Some individuals will deny that they house such evil. According to the Freudian account adopted and developed by Jung and Peterson, this is because human minds also have a highly socialized self-conscious portion that strives to cover up what dwells in its dark basement. We spend a lot of time thinking about the person we wish we were, but we do not spend much time thinking about the person we actually are, faults and all. However, because Peterson's inquiry starts from an experiential baseline, anyone taking this approach must honestly take stock of whatever they find, without prejudging it. Peterson contends that if we listen to the dialogues taking place within us, we will discern some disturbing voices.

As Peterson became more attentive to what was going on inside his mind, he catalogued episodes such as the following. As a student attending classes, he 'would unfailingly feel the urge to stab the point of my pen into the neck of the person in front of me' (1999, p. xvi). Peterson did not view himself as having a violent disposition. But, sometime prior, as part of his studies in psychology, he had 'visited a maximum security prison [...] full of murderers, rapists and armed robbers' (1999, p. xv). There, he'd had a pleasant conversation with a 'harmless-appearing little man' who, it turned out, 'had murdered two policemen after he had forced them to dig their own graves' (1999, p. xvi). This first-hand encounter left Peterson with a nagging doubt: if a normal-looking person is capable of such an abominable act, how can we be certain that, just because we seem normal, no similar evil lurks inside us?

Confronting this possibility head-on, Peterson 'tried to imagine, *really imagine*, what I would have to be like to do such a thing' (1999, p. xvi). His conclusion was that we are all nearer to evil acts than we would like to think. 'The truly appalling aspect of such atrocity did not lie in its impossibility or remoteness, as I had naïvely assumed, but in its *ease*. I was not much different from the violent prisoners—not *qualitatively* different. I could do what they could do (although I hadn't)' (1999, p. xvi). We experience emotions, but the cause of those emotions is not always obvious. Peterson's classroom fantasies were a symptom of his attempt to come to terms with this disturbing possibility.

Peterson's discovery of his own potential evil plunged him into a period of self-doubt. The experience nevertheless forced him to realize that we each contain multiple voices talking at cross purposes. Some voice blurts out something embarrassing and, all of a sudden, another voice intervenes to insist that no, 'You don't believe that. That isn't true' (Peterson 1999, p. xvii). Practising something similar to what Buddhists call mindfulness, Peterson sat back and listened to the exchanges within him. He resolved to gradually gain control of the conversation: 'I tried only to say things that my internal reviewer would pass unchallenged. This meant that I really had to listen to what I was saying, that I spoke much less often, and that I would frequently stop, midway through a sentence, feel embarrassed, and reformulate my thoughts' (1999, p. xvii). This disciplined regimen of honesty eventually paid off, since 'I soon noticed that I felt much less agitated and more confident when I only said things that the "voice" did not object to' (1999, p. xvii). In effect, Peterson was learning how to follow his *conscience*.

The idea of a moral conscience can be explained without resorting to anything supernatural. We are rational animals, so our animal impulses are combined with a species-specific ability to monitor what we think, say, and do. As Jung explained, 'we cannot simply abstain from judgment. If we call good something that seems to us bad, we have in effect told a lie' (1960, p. 92). When you lie silently, you think no one notices, but *you* notice, and in the end that is what matters most.

One of the darkest thoughts you can have is envy. As the Russian-American philosopher and novelist Ayn Rand pointed out:

Envy is regarded by most people as a petty, superficial emotion and, therefore, it serves as a semihuman cover for so inhuman an emotion that those who feel it seldom dare admit it even to themselves […]. That emotion is: *hatred of the good for being the good*. This hatred is not resentment against some prescribed view of the good with which one does not agree […]. Hatred of the good for being the good means hatred of that which one regards as good by one's own (conscious or subconscious) judgment. It means hatred of a person for possessing a value or virtue one regards as desirable. If a child wants to get good grades in school, but is unable or unwilling to achieve them and begins to hate the children who do, that is hatred of the good. If a man regards intelligence as a value, but is troubled by self-doubt and begins to hate the men he judges to be intelligent, that is hatred of the good. [...] The primary factor and distinguishing characteristic is an emotional mechanism set in reverse: a response of hatred, not toward human vices, but toward human virtues. (Rand 1999, p. 152)

Peterson suggests that some of the worst atrocities of the twentieth century were driven not by a love of the poor, but by a hatred of the rich and success generally (Peterson 2018a, p. 288–90). This emotion is too disturbing to accept, so it is cloaked by a mock emotion that pretends to espouse noble ideals. More often than not, though, revolutionaries who smash windows just want to smash windows.

Now, one might object that because Peterson's account posits self-deception, it is not falsifiable. However, some facts allow us to infer the presence of something akin to hatred of the good for being the good. To see this, one needs only to ask a pair of questions. First, have collectivist schemes to help the poor in fact helped the poor? Second, have collectivist schemes to help the poor been abandoned? The answer to both questions is no. So why are people still pushing grand social schemes we know to be destructive? Peterson's psychological analysis helps to explain this bizarre political fact.

According to Peterson, we have motives so dark that we dare not admit to having them. One of those dark motives is the desire to destroy successful and happy people—even if no positive consequence follows from that destruction. The most extreme case of this is murder-suicide. By definition, the person who caps her murdering spree with a suicide cannot possibility gain anything from the carnage. Peterson rejects the hypothesis that such an action is inexplicable. The phenomenon does have an explanation, only this explanation points to a segment of the experiential spectrum too disturbing to be acknowledged.

Peterson observes that when mass killings happen, 'Everyone says "We don't understand"' (2018a, p. 150). Yet the truth is that those who perpetrate murder-suicides are often open about the nature of their hatred, leaving behind well-documented statements of their motives and intent. Despite this, 'we will not listen, because the truth cuts too close to the bone' (2018a, p. 150).

It may well be that inside you there is a strand of resentment similar to that experienced by the Columbine High School killers. Thankfully, you will not act out this dark sentiment in so gruesome a manner. Even so, with the right context—such as the privacy of a voting booth, or the anonymity of an angry mob—your dark motives can find an outlet. The first step to immunizing yourself is accepting that you are fully capable of having genuinely evil motives. Your espousal of a given ideology might not be driven by the noble motives you credit yourself with.

Naturally, many people will resist Peterson's analysis or at any rate find it misplaced. 'Surely', the typical reply goes, 'all this talk of envy and resentment is not applicable to *me*'. Such a response, however, might be the best indicator that Peterson's psychological analysis is onto something. You are not all good. But you are not all evil either. Rather, as Jung says: 'Confronting a man with his shadow means showing him his own light. Once one has experienced a few times what it is like to stand judgingly between the opposites, one begins to understand what is meant by the self. Anyone who perceives his shadow and his light simultaneously sees himself from two sides and thus gets in the middle' (Jung 1960, p. 96).

Chapter 10

Summary

Here you are—this much is given. Additionally, you are not alone, since the very fact that you are deciphering these letters attests to your immersion in a language, society, and culture. A language presupposes multiple persons. So it turns out that I am here too. You are presently decoding what I encoded. However, the human-made cultural sphere that binds us does not exhaust reality, since it is, in turn, capped by the natural world. Despite massive advances in science, nature is mostly unexplored (think of exoplanets), so it is bordered by a boundless expanse of unknown lands. There are thus concentric rings radiating outward: you, culture, nature, and the unknown. Each of these domains has some good and bad in it, in so far as a person can be a hero or a villain, living among others can be liberating or oppressive, nature can nourish or threaten, and the unknown can house both pleasant and unpleasant surprises. This, in sum, is Peterson's full map of the world.

Of course, the word 'map' is used loosely here, since what Peterson aims to chart are not land masses and bodies of water, but fundamental varieties of human experience.

In a time when most academics favour piecemeal analyses, Peterson is trying to unite various theories in a way that sheds light on the human condition as a whole. To achieve this, he draws on the pervasive phenomenon of ignorance. Since human existence is goal-directed and since problems force us to imagine new solutions, one broad but true claim we can make is that '[w]e constantly compare the world at present to the world idealized in fantasy, render affective judgment, and act in consequence' (Peterson 1999, p. 27). No organism can claim final mastery over its environment, so the basic categories of chaos and order have been hammered into the very fabric of our bodies, from our earliest ancestors onward.

The world beyond what we currently know is for us to discover, not invent. Still, individuals have some leeway in choosing where they are heading. To help us cope with the unknown and integrate discoveries in a way that makes our lives better, we need the guidance of stories. The most enduring narrative patterns, then, are those that offer a recipe (and inspiration) for how to overcome adversity and challenges.

A strength of Peterson's synthetic undertaking is that it respects the explanatory and predictive power of the natural and social sciences while at the same time acknowledging that these recent achievements sit atop a far longer history of myth making.

> [O]ur ancestors understood metaphorically at least five thousand years ago that the process of creative courageous encounter with the unknown comprised the central process underlying successful human adaptation, and that this process stood as the veritable precondition for the existence and maintenance of all good things. Such understanding, however, was implicit and low-resolution—at best, procedural, embodied, encoded in ritual and drama—and not something elaborated to the point we would consider explicit or semantic understanding today. (Peterson and Flanders 2002, p. 453)

Owing to this long history, some patterns essential to biological survival have become ingrained in our cultural practices and psyches. So, when we zoom out, we see humanity telling and retelling stories that have considerable overlap. The modern scientific mindset misinterprets these ancient myths when it glosses them as (false) descriptions of the world, since they are in fact blueprints for how to act.

Culture, on this view, is by definition familiar, since it is a web of conventions and practices woven by humans to coordinate their individual actions and collective undertakings. Culture preserves and promulgates whatever measure of order and security humans have managed to construct over the centuries. Nature, by contrast, can never be fully tamed by our cultural understandings, so it always retains an element of mystery. A good story is one that does justice to the relative benefits and limitations of both culture and nature, while a meaningful life is one that gets the dosage of familiarity and exposure to the unknown just right.

It takes a significant degree of abstraction for human animals to properly picture their place in the grand scheme of things. Still, in order to properly orient oneself in the world (i.e. decide what to *do*), it is imperative that one represent that world in some rudimentary way. Since this task cannot be avoided, Peterson believes that a low-resolution map of the human condition has been formulated and refined by generations of storytellers. Of course, this historical claim cannot be fully verified; beyond a certain point, '[w]e do not know what our ancestors were talking about' (1999, p. 8). Peterson must therefore ground his theorizing only in features that every human in every circumstance faced.

Confronting the unknown is one of those features. Another thing we can say for certain is that every person had two parents. Peterson uses this fact to make a trivially true observation and an ambitious suggestion. The trivially true observation is that 'parents serve as primary intermediaries of culture: *they embody language in their behavior* and transmit it to [their child] during their day-to-day activities' (1999, p. 93). Peterson suggests more ambitiously that instead of developing separate representational systems for known/unknown and father/ mother pairs, we used one system to explain the other. This generated a host of allegories that still shape our thinking.

What we call myths are in fact descriptions of the biological predicament (e.g. threat, reward, struggle, etc.), couched in more familiar and captivating narrative terms (e.g. dragons, treasures, epic battles, etc.). Biological life cannot afford the luxury of excess, so '[w]hen something evolves, it must build upon what nature has already produced' (Peterson 2018a, p. 11). Human symbolism will thus tend to piggyback on interpretative strategies that have proven their worth. Symbolism that proves its worth becomes archetypal. One important consequence of Peterson's evolutionary account is that if a cultural practice is preserved for generations, then that practice must have benefitted us in some way — otherwise it would have been pruned long ago. We should not disregard behavioural adaptations that have served humans for millennia.

According to the symbolism catalogued by Peterson, '[t]he Great Mother [...] is the unpredictable', whereas 'the Great Father is the tyrant who forbids the emergence [...] of anything new' (1999, p. 105). These metaphors are layered atop a preexisting biological division. But in Peterson's complete account, this duality is (and must be) constantly traversed by an active third party who lives on the dividing line between the *yin* of innovative chaos and the *yang* of established order (1999, p. 104; for a restatement of this three-part view in psychological terms, see Peterson 2004). Peterson's account thus gives centre stage to the freethinker who seeks to steer a tenable path between dogmatic closure and dogmatic openness:

> Anything that protects and fosters (and that is therefore predictable and powerful) necessarily has the capacity to smother and oppress (and may manifest those capacities, unpredictably, in any given situation). No static political

utopia is therefore possible [...]. Recognition of the essentially ambivalent nature of the predictable—stultifying but secure—means discarding simplistic theories which attribute the existence of human suffering and evil purely to the state, or which presume that the state is all that is good, and that the individual should exist merely as subordinate or slave. (Peterson 1999, pp. 214–15)

According to this picture, the central goal of a healthy society is not to solve a particular problem but rather to curate open channels of deliberation that foster problem solving in general. That is why Peterson gives centre stage to speech. Commenting on the Evergreen State College hostage taking, Bret Weinstein says (in a documentary by Mike Nayna): 'This isn't about free speech and this is only tangentially about college campuses. This is about a breakdown in the basic logic of civilization.' Language is not a way to repackage ready-made thoughts. Rather, it is what enables thought itself to take shape. So when dialogue is stifled, the activity of thinking is stifled.

Dogmatic belief systems and political regimes want to stifle independent thought by banning the free expression of ideas. Genuine heterodoxy can be maintained by heeding the call to not block the way of inquiry (Peirce 1931–58, vol. 1, para. 135). Personality types each have their own blind spots, so it makes sense for a well-working society to encourage viewpoint diversity. Dissenters are rarely pleasant to contend with. But if ideas indeed spread by processes akin to natural selection, then a person holding a dissenting view is what evolutionary theorists call a 'hopeful monster' (Goldschmidt 1940, p. 390) — an organism possessing a minority trait that may well spread in the long run. A life plagued by ignorance and suffering is hard enough, so we don't need to curtail potential solutions by excluding viewpoints and shutting down maverick minds.

Finding solutions to problems is hard, so amid the uncertain turmoil of real life we need to refer ourselves to ideals. Ideals range over any conceivable person and action and in this sense are universal. Peterson holds that when we move away from universal systems of belief such as religion, we move away from time-tested insights about how to face adversity. Hence, there is much to gain from surveying the stores of wisdom that we implicitly rely on in our daily affairs.

Such a survey, Peterson argues, will reveal that many superstitious beliefs once had a plausible basis. For instance, the most natural way to explain many phenomena is to ascribe to them the various personalities that we are best acquainted with. Historically, this projection of psychology onto nature resulted in a plurality of deities. According to Peterson, the progression from polytheism to monotheism embodies a collective reflection on which values ought to be regarded as supreme. The chief advantage afforded by a monotheist con-ception, according to Peterson, is that it lets us appreciate how 'all members of the species *Homo sapiens* are essentially equivalent, equal before God: we find ourselves vulnerable, mortal creatures, thrown into a universe bent on our creation and protection—and our transformation and destruction' (1999, p. 108). The most productive way to view belief in God, then, is not as a theoretical commitment to his existence but rather as a pragmatic commitment to the individualist ideals that he symbolically exemplifies.

Because limitations in resources mean that not all valuable activities can be pursued, we need to compare our options and figure out which are more valuable. Sometimes this com-parison takes place on an individual scale, but larger-scale patterns like markets and animal groups also manage to arrange goods and services in a hierarchical structure. Since the goal of hierarchies is to maximize the good, Peterson thinks it is simplistic and misguided to regard all hierarchies as symptoms of oppressive forces. Genuine oppression can certainly happen (slavery, for example). However, those who view everything through the lens of power likely do so because of a desire to evade their own envy and to eschew personal responsibility.

One does not have to travel to an exoplanet to come face to face with the unknown. In fact, any nearby person necessarily has aspects that escape us. That is why it is so important to treat each person as an individual. When we categorize another person according to some surface feature, such as skin colour, we adopt a one-size-fits-all template that artificially expunges the chaos housed in that person. Unpredictability is annoying and listening is hard, so it is tempting to use groups as the basic units of analysis. There is no need to learn from someone by conversing once we have rendered that person entirely predictable. According to Peterson, this group-based approach is exactly 'what *totalitarian* means: Everything that needs to be discovered has been discovered. Everything will unfold precisely as planned. All problems will vanish, forever, once the perfect system is accepted' (2018a, p. 218). In a flash, the group-based approach explains all social ills: *these* people are to blame. The simplistic explanation of a multifaceted phenomenon is the hallmark of an ideology (Peterson and Flanders 2002, pp. 454–55). However, Peterson insists that 'the truth is neither a collection of slogans nor an ideology. It will instead be personal' (2018a, p. 230). This individualist credo requires a standing readiness to revise one's beliefs in light of new evidence. Instead of peddling ideologies, educational systems should strive to make students antifragile. Leading by example, teachers should make their pupils strong enough to engage with genuinely different viewpoints and to deal with each other as individuals, not as instances of some predictable category.

Peterson's critique of ideological possession has struck a nerve. Let me therefore propose a conceptual framework that can clarify his stance. The psychological anthropologist Richard Shweder and his colleagues (Shweder *et al.* 1997) conducted studies that led them to identify three major sources of strong moral sentiments. Jonathan Haidt, who worked with Shweder, summarizes these sources as follows:

> The ethic of *autonomy* is based on the idea that people are, first and foremost, autonomous individuals with wants, needs, and preferences. People should be free to satisfy these wants, needs, and preferences as they see fit, and so societies develop moral concepts such as rights, liberty, and justice, which allow people to coexist peacefully without interfering too much in each other's projects. [...]
>
> The ethic of *community* is based on the idea that people are, first and foremost, members of larger entities such as families, teams, armies, companies, tribes, and nations. These larger entities are more than the sum of the people who compose them; they are real, they matter, and they must be protected. People have an obligation to play their assigned roles in these entities. [...]
>
> The ethic of *divinity* is based on the idea that people are, first and foremost, temporary vessels within which a divine soul has been implanted. People are not just animals with an extra serving of consciousness; they are children of God and should behave accordingly. [...] Many societies therefore develop moral concepts such as sanctity and sin, purity and pollution, elevation and degradation. (Haidt 2012, pp. 116–17)

These three moralities are major players on the world stage. Not only do they drive what people do, they figure in the reasons people give to justify what they do. The moralities serve as the starting point of anyone's thinking. It is not as if parents or guardians refrain from imparting ethical behaviour to their children, raise them in a neutral vacuum, and then ask their children to pick their code of conduct upon reaching adulthood. What happens instead is that people inherit their morality from their parents or guardians, who inherited it from their parents, and so on. This chain of replication illustrates Peterson's claim that while people die, the patterns of their stories survive.

Using Shweder's conceptual scaffold, here is what I think Peterson contributes to these issues:

1) He shows how the moralities that people inherit from their culture influence their thoughts, feelings, and actions in all sorts of ways.

2) He clarifies how the main conveyor belts of (1) are narrative archetypes.

3) He uses the archetypes of (2) to (re)construct a historical lineage for the ethic of autonomy, showing it to be a hard-earned result that goes back much farther than the Enlightenment.

4) He uses the account of (3) to provide an autonomy-friendly portrayal of the ethic of divinity by arguing that the individual can be seen as divine.

5) He uses a mixture of historical events and psychological analysis to explain how, when the insights of (4) are forgotten, an ethic of community can lead to groupthink, and an ethic of divinity can lead to dogmatism.

6) He reminds us of how easily the groupthink and dogmatism of (5) can descend into mindless violence.

7) Despite the critique levelled in (6), he stresses that human fallibility requires an open and constant dialogue between the different ethics, each of which has something to offer.

8) He argues that while an ethic of divinity should be our main ideal (*pace* claim 4), and conversation is a communal act (*pace* claim 7), an ethic of autonomy is the methodological prerequisite for any dialogue, in so far as every individual must be left free to think for themselves and speak their mind.

Looking at these contributions synoptically, it is no wonder that Peterson has garnered so much attention. Here is how, two decades removed from its publication, Peterson summarizes his most important work:

> I proposed in *Maps of Meaning* that the great myths and religious stories of the past, particularly those derived from an earlier, oral tradition, were *moral* in their intent, rather than descriptive. Thus, they did not concern themselves with what the world was, as a scientist might have it, but with how a human being should act. I suggested that our ancestors portrayed the world as a stage—a drama— instead of a place of objects. I described how I had come to believe that the constituent elements of the world as drama were order and chaos, and not material things. (Peterson 2018a, p. xxvii)

Against this backdrop, Peterson articulates a vision where 'the soul of the individual eternally hungers for the heroism of genuine Being' and where 'the willingness to take on that responsibility is identical to the decision to live a meaningful life' (2018a, pp. xxxiv–xxxv).

The world is an increasingly confused and confusing one, but it doesn't have to be. To those who want to fight evil, Peterson says: 'Don't blame capitalism, the radical left, or the iniquity of your enemies' (2018a, p. 158). Instead, his recommendation is to start fighting the evil within you. That should keep you busy. It might also decrease the facile tendency to view the world as a struggle between 'us' and 'them' (whoever 'they' are).

Everybody clamours for large-scale change (whatever that means). Yet if the world is ever going to improve, it will be by virtue of individuals improving themselves. Peterson's goal is to provide a general road map for such personal improvement. This, at any rate, is the story that he is telling. As with all stories, we can ask whether it is any good. Peterson's account may or may not be life-enhancing. But the precondition for evaluating a story is the ability to tell it.

Part 2

Evaluation

Chapter 11

Were religious insights arrived at by induction or revelation?

Peterson's training in the social sciences allows him to down-play — or at least render less mystical — the religious aspect of religion. Indeed, 'Peterson reconceptualizes the Genesis stories as a kind of primordial self-help book. Abraham's story of sacrifice becomes a lesson in delayed gratification. The flood becomes a metaphor for surviving the tragedies and trials of life', and, as Peterson paces onstage, 'something overtly political like class resentment will get smuggled into the Cain and Abel story' (Beckner 2018, p. 28). Interpretations like these can have some value, but they usually require semantic gymnastics that, were they applied to other fields, would cripple inquiry.

Take, for example, Peterson's interpretation of how the Ten Commandments came about. The Old Testament tells us that this list was dictated to Moses by a booming voice coming from a burning bush. Clearly, no serious social scientist should take this story literally (or, if a social scientist were to accept the story, it would be as a subjective report of some hallucination, lie, or delusion). Peterson thus gives the old story a new spin. On his telling, Moses got his commandments not by revelation, but by induction.

Induction is what happens when one takes many instances and generalizes some overarching conclusion from them. To pick an ordinary example, if you observe that every time there are apples in your garbage bags, these bags get torn by raccoons, your accumulated observations allow you to arrive at a general lesson that *whenever* apples are in the bags, raccoons will tear them. Inductive inferences range over more than what was strictly observed, since they implicitly make predictions about events that have yet to happen. This prediction is not 100 percent certain, since it could be that, one day, you put out the trash with apples, but raccoons don't feast on them. Induction thus allows us to draw probable but falsifiable conclusions. Although falsifiability is missing from religious conviction, Peterson argues that when Moses descended from Mount Sinai with commandments, he essentially presented his fellow tribes-people with the fruits of an induction.

Peterson notes that for years Moses adjudicated people's disputes. Folks would come to him with grievances, and he would decide who was right. As Peterson recounts, '[i]n the course of the exodus, Moses begins to serve as judge for his people. [...] In this role, he is forced to determine what was right, or what should be—and what was wrong, or compara-tively wrong' (1999, p. 375). This experience as mediator gave Moses first-hand exposure to ethical matters. Of course, each dispute is unique. Still, if we leave out the details, we can discern common traits in various wrongdoings. Stealing some-one's cow, for instance, is essentially the same as stealing some-one's goat. Likewise, as a general pattern, the act of breaking a promise stays the same, irrespective of the content of the promise. According to Peterson, Moses and others before him must have been slowly figuring out what all these similarities were.

Peterson's account fits with 'the documentary hypothesis', which takes significant portions of the Bible to have been collectively authored (see Baden 2012, pp. 13–33). In Peterson's gloss, the Ten Commandments encapsulate in words not so much what a supernatural being dictated, but what humans learned. Moses and his peers who wrote the Bible were not social scientists, since they relied on regular observation instead of questionnaires and other controlled methods (Peterson 2018a, p. 102). But given that humans had been acting morally (and immorally) long before the Ten Commandments, Moses 'transform[ed] what had previously been custom, embedded in behavior, represented in myth, into an explicit semantic code' (Peterson 1999, p. 377).

Peterson conjectures that when this simmering process of reflection boiled over into Moses's mind as a series of verbal statements, it felt like a revelation. According to this psychological account, there was nothing mystical about the event. Moses was using a vast sample of observations of people's behaviour to formulate core principles that, in the long run, best promote a stable society. When trying to fathom large abstractions, the conscious mind works in tandem with the unconscious. Since there is no single instance that one can point to in order to justify the objective basis of a very large-scale pattern, stories about booming voices and burning bushes were an allegorical way to express Moses's grasp of profound insights.

The Petersonian reconstruction of the Old Testament story is certainly more attractive than an undiluted appeal to supernatural revelation. The problem, though, is that from a textual standpoint the commandments conveyed by Moses do not appeal to induction. Importantly, an induction is an inference that can be justified by evidence. If one asks why you think raccoons will tear up the garbage bags tonight, you can back up that forecast with a body of tangible observations. Your belief in what will happen rests on events that have in fact happened.

All of this is verifiable (a video could record the raccoons) and even testable (predictions can fail to happen). The same cannot be said of the Commandments. One can, if one wishes, justify a prescription such as 'You shall not murder' by highlighting that following this rule has in the past led to a more stable society. Yet the fact is that this argumentative support is not offered in the Old Testament.

Of course, some religious scholars would insist that the Ten Commandments enjoy argumentative support. According to Mark Glouberman, 'the Bible's manner of composition suggests that the composers see the God-based motivations connected with the first five commandments as underpinning the imperatives of the second set' (2019, p. 80). Glouberman thus reads the Decalogue as two Pentalogues. This structure allows for some sort of justification: 'Why is killing wrong? Why should you not steal? I'll tell you why. The Lord is God' (Glouberman 2019, p. 80). So while Glouberman does not think the first commandment entails the others, he does claim that as 'the chief religious commandment, [it] *underpins* the rest' (2019, p. 80). This gloss may satisfy the demand for some justification. But justification is an activity that can (and should) be iterated, so even if the sixth commandment is justified by the first commandment, we can legitimately ask what justifies the first. Glouberman could insist that 'The Lord is God' is an axiom, but since he repudiates the idea that the first five commandments deductively entail the following five, taking one commandment as an axiom would not allow him to generate the others in an axiomatic-deductive fashion.

Peterson certainly cannot claim that the moral insights of the Bible are self-evident, since he presents those insights as the hard-earned result of millions of years of trial and error, from lobsters to current-day humans. Indeed, according to him, '[t]he Bible has been thrown up, out of the deep, by the collective human imagination, which is itself a product of unimaginable forces operating over unfathomable spans of time' (Peterson 2018a, p. 104). Evolutionary considerations may explain why communities of humans are bound to eventually converge on certain norms like prohibitions of murder. Yet Peterson's attempt to justify the Ten Commandments on inductive grounds becomes less plausible when we consider prescriptions such as 'Remember the Sabbath day, to keep it holy'. If, as Peterson says, generalizations become 'truer' the more observations we take into consideration, will this reverence for the seventh day of the week still hold when we factor in all world cultures?

I do not question that human beings can (and often do) arrive at moral insights long before they can verbally state them. I also do not question that, psychologically, this sudden ability to verbally state a moral insight can feel like a revelation. I wholeheartedly agree with Peterson that a moral intuition is better when stated, since '[t]he benefits of its abstraction — communicability and potential for rapid generalization — make it a potent force for the establishment and continuation of order' (1999, p. 387). Yet stating a moral insight is far less demanding (and far less informative) than *justifying* that insight. As things stand, the Ten Commandments provide no reason(s) for why they should be followed.

Of course, noting that reasons are absent in Moses's tablets does not mean that no reasons could be given. Presumably, Peterson is attempting to do just that. Still, even if we accept Peterson's speculative suggestion that Moses distilled decades of judicial experience (and millennia of cultural adaptations), it nevertheless remains that Moses couched his insights in the imperative mood. Their name says it all: it is the Ten *Commandments*, not the ten observations.

If they were the ten observations, they would be justified and could be revised. As things stand, the Commandments are neither justified nor revisable. So Peterson can keep his inductive account and drop his religious commitments, or keep his religious commitments and drop his inductive account.

My portrayal of Peterson's views is incomplete, since he contends that '[Christ] pushes morality beyond strict reliance on codified tradition—the explicit Law of Moses' (1999, p. 385). Peterson notes that '[l]ike Moses [...] Christ delivers his most famous address [...] on a mountaintop' (1999, p. 387). But since Christ will claim to be not just the mouthpiece of God, but the *son* of God, attempts to replace divine authority with inductive generalization become even more implausible in the New Testament. Indeed, most Christians would agree that '[t]o adhere to Christian imperatives in our late modern age must mean more than improving our being. It must mean believing in God as if he were really there and treating the Bible as if it were really true' (Ashford 2020, p. 24).

The Ten Commandments were not arrived at by repeated observations. Or, if they were, we are never told what those observations were. If we could assess those observations, we would know under what conditions the moral prescriptions could be shown to be false. A commandment, however, cannot be 'wrong'. 'Do fifty push-ups' is liable of being obeyed or disobeyed, but it is in itself neither true nor false (although 'Marc did nine push-ups' is). Given that the imperative mood is not amenable to further scrutiny, scientific or mundane, it makes no difference that 'the Law of Moses is based upon prohibition, description of what is forbidden: "Thou shalt not"', whereas 'Christ's message is more in the manner of exhortation, description of active good: "Thou shalt...."' (Peterson 1999, p. 387, see Frye 1982, pp. 131–32). In either case, if one has the audacity to ask *why*, one essentially meets with the same response: because some supernatural entity said so.

One could reply that some of the Bible's stories and narratives provide examples of what befalls people when they do not follow its laws. This, the reply would go, provides some weak inductive justification. The reply is sensible. However, if the ills that accompany disobedience come from God, then their source is supernatural; and if they come from elsewhere (normal floods, say), then their source is natural—so these events can no longer count as 'punishments'.

Peterson's argument is thus subject to the following dilemma. The teachings of the Bible can be justified either by mystical means (revelation) or by empirical means (induction). If they can be justified by mystical means, then Peterson must explain why this particular body of teachings should be privileged over others. One cannot dodge this by saying that all religious texts agree on the basics. If that were the case, we would not be facing the kind of deep disagreements that prompt Peterson to take a stand. Likewise, preferential treatment of the Judeo-Christian tradition cannot appeal to a head-count of disciples and/or divine insight, since both strategies could be used by Peterson's religious rivals to prop up their preferred text.

If, on the other hand, the teachings of the Bible can be justified by empirical means, as Peterson claims they can, then we need to be told in a non-circular way why some actions and not others were singled out as praiseworthy. I do not think that this can be done. But even if the demand for a non-circular explanation were met, it would mean that the Bible is note-worthy only in the non-devotional way that history (and not theology) already deems it. Peterson is tautologically right that '[c]odification of tradition is necessarily dependent upon existence of tradition' (1999, p. 377). Yet to the extent that this is right, the source of moral guidance is tradition, not religion. So if Peterson is correct that 'established adaptive behavior' (1999, p. 377) is 'hierarchically structured as a consequence of quasi-Darwinian competition' (1999, p. 378), then the evolutionary elements have completely supplanted the religious elements.

Call this the Stone Soup Objection—to parallel the folk tale about a soup that was allegedly made from a stone but in fact got all its flavour from the other ingredients added to it.

The Stone Soup Objection essentially asks: if moral norms can be known without any faith in the Bible, then why not simply forgo faith in the Bible? To my mind, Peterson is at his best when he stresses that one's individual life matters and one's nature is in part to be rational. I am delighted to see these tenets being re-introduced into the (otherwise relativist and collectivist) debates. Peterson only goes astray when he tries to force those tenets into a religious idiom. This may not be fatal, since in practice what Peterson means by 'religious' is 'of ultimate value'. What stands in need of explanation, then, is the fact that what Peterson has to say is intelligible and potentially persuasive even when one has not read his recommended text, the Bible. This suggests that an evidence-based account of ultimate value can be defended independently, without invoking the problematic authority of religion.

The Ten Commandments were revealed by God, not observed from people's behaviour. This is how most religious people see it, anyway. Peterson is free to gloss his preferred religious text in a way that eschews revelation and turns its narrative teachings into a psychological outgrowth of repeated observations. Nothing prevents such an inductive account from being persuasive. But we should be clear that, at that point, one is buying into Jordan Peterson's ideas, not the Bible.

One way to bring clarity to the situation is to consider the following stances, arranged according to their quantifiers: (a) *all* that is in the Bible is true and/or worthwhile; (b) *most* of what is in the Bible is true and/or worthwhile; or (c) *some* of what is in the Bible is true and/or worthwhile.

Peterson would reject stance (a), which would sound too openly fundamentalist for his ears. Likewise, stance (c) is almost guaranteed to be correct, albeit trivially so. Surely any text rooted in history is bound to get *something* right (since the reverse, getting everything wrong, would be quite unlikely). Peterson thus provides reasons for taking stance (b) more seriously than a scientific orientation would otherwise recommend. Indeed, many atheists and secular thinkers who would normally reject stance (b) have been moved by Peterson to rethink how much in the Bible is true and/or worthwhile. Yet, in defending stance (b), Peterson appeals to flexible interpretations that are essentially predicated on stance (a), which says that *all* that is in the Bible is true and/or worthwhile.

Let us look at one particularly salient illustration of such flexible interpretations. Midway through the Joe Rogan podcast number 1070, Peterson brings up the New Testament's claim that '[t]he meek shall inherit the earth' (Matthew 5:5). As he explains, 'There is something wrong with that line. It just doesn't make sense to me. Meek just doesn't seem to me to be a moral virtue'. Indeed, the passage about the meek coming on top sounds like a bumper sticker for 'equity' (i.e. equality of outcome). Now, a genuine advocate of stance (b) who repudiates equity could have simply taken this as an indication that the statement in question is wrong. However, when it comes to the Bible, Peterson's reflex is charity verging on credulity. Apart from flatly counterfactual claims (about the Earth being at the centre of the universe, and so on), he rarely lets anything go. Hence, anyone uncomfortable with the ethical implications of the religious verse can start to toy with alternative word meanings in order to obtain the message they desire.

Standard synonyms of 'meek' include 'gentle', 'easily imposed on', and 'submissive'. Like Nietzsche, Peterson (2018a, pp. 318–26) regards these traits as vices, not virtues. So to reconcile this with the Bible he looks for more esoteric etymologies. The word 'meek' supposedly comes from the Greek word *'praus'*, which alludes to strength under control. By the time Peterson is done with his semantic massage, the verse about the 'meek' has come to mean (in Peterson's words): 'Those who have swords and know how to use them but keep them sheathed will inherit the world' (Joe Rogan podcast 1070). All of a sudden, Jesus sounds like someone who would have been pals with Nietzsche.

Commenting on this move from 'meek' to 'those who have weapons', Peterson says: 'That's a lot different, man. It's a lot

better' (Biblical Series IX: The Call to Abraham). Different?
Clearly. Better? Perhaps. But *by what standard*?

Peterson does not hunt for such replacements for every
word in the Bible—only for those that do not fit his individualist outlook. Etymology and philological scholarship can
thus be switched on or off, to fit one's particular needs. In this
way, the conflict in Peterson's religious and philosophical
commitments, which initially made him question the literal
meaning of the Biblical verse, can be conveniently ironed out.

Peterson informs us that he went on a website called Bible
Hub and found his alternative meaning there. What he doesn't
tell us is that the passage about the meek comes right after
another verse that says 'Blessed are the poor in spirit, for theirs
is the kingdom of heaven' (Matthew 5:3). This clearly supports
the interpretation according to which meek simply means
meek. I suppose that, with enough patience and ingenuity, the
expression 'poor in spirit' can also be reconciled with antifragility. Since the Bible cannot say which interpretation is best,
such interpretations are guided by something *other* than the
Bible. You can see whatever you want in an inkblot, but
pointing at it to justify what (you think) you see is unhelpful.

When we shop around for a meaning that suits us, what are
we doing, exactly? Do we bounce among the various words,
unsure which one we will settle on—or do we start with a prior
sense of what we are looking for, hoping to find some historical
rationalization for what we already believe? It seems to me that
Peterson has already decided what he wants the Bible to teach
him.

Going against the obvious, Peterson says, '[m]eek does not
mean meek' (Biblical Series IX: The Call to Abraham). From an
epistemological standpoint, such a permissive (and oddly postmodern) about-face is disastrous. Imagine what would happen
if, when trying to assess a biological account, 'turtle' did not
mean 'turtle'. Fallible inquiry is a difficult activity, so we can
have productive disagreements about whether a claim is true

or false, good or bad. There are many roads alongside the highway of literal interpretation. But when a given claim is capable of making a complete U-turn, there is no possibility of eventually reaching a principled agreement (Eco 1990).

Like many Peterson fans who have not read about Peterson's grandmother stroking his face with her pubic hairs —'I looked at her ruined face and said, "Yes, Grandma, it's soft"' (Peterson 1999, p. 164) — many Christians have never read the Bible. At one point in that text (Numbers 31:17-18), God orders his disciples to kill an entire population — except the virgin girls, whom the disciples can keep. There are instructions on how to purchase and keep slaves (Leviticus 25:44-46) and when to publicly stone to death a disobedient child (Deuteronomy 21:18-21). Are we to do an interpretive rescue operation for all these stories? The episode with the pubic hairs was just a dream, the stuff about the virgins was just to test the character of believers, stoning a child was just a metaphor, and so on. Such interpretations are certainly available. If we indulge in them, though, we leave ourselves little ground to stand on when the time comes to take a passage seriously.

Peterson's attempt to rationalize the belief systems that he was exposed to as a child with the more realistic convictions he adopted as an adult has triggered productive conversations about topics that have been neglected, such as individual responsibility, the role of tradition, and so on. Still, the Bible can be interpreted in various ways. As Ron Dart observes, 'students who have come from Wiccan and Gnostic traditions […] tend to see the God who ordered Adam and Eve not to eat from the tree as an authoritarian tyrant and Adam and Eve using their agency to be free from such a bully. How is the myth of Eden to be read, and how do we know which reading is best?' (Dart 2020, p. 79). I do not know how to adjudicate such competing interpretations. If we exclude empty posturing, no one else knows either.

Peterson is free to say, if he wants, that restrained power is a virtuous thing. After all, the Sermon on the Mount was not humanity's last chance to say something informative about morality. Yet Peterson essentially uses Jesus as a hand puppet to present his own views. For those raised in a Christian setting, this rhetorical technique gives his pronouncements a special appeal. But the appeal to authority can easily backfire. Indeed, what if a true believer were to insist, quite forcefully, that what Jesus meant by 'meek' is exactly the traditional sense of 'gentle', 'easily imposed on', and 'submissive'. How would *that* debate unfold? Since both sides can cherry-pick the meanings that serve them best, the only way to resolve whether meekness is a virtue is to provide *arguments* for one's view. We know how to evaluate those (see Kelley 2014; Hicks and Kelley 1998; or any number of critical thinking textbooks).

Peterson insists that we miss the point when we fixate on the allegedly supernatural origins of documents such as the Bible. On his telling, religious prescriptions codify flashes of human insight that were in fact the product of repeated social observations. This is no doubt true. After all, *some* of what is in the Bible is true and worthwhile. But in the long run, Peterson does a disservice to his views by expounding them via the Bible. It is probably best, then, to avoid the quicksand of religious interpretation and stay on firm argumentative terrain. The Bible is, like the Quran or the Torah, a human-made document—nothing more, nothing less. So when one finds something in these (no longer sacred) texts that is not true or not worthwhile, it's okay to let it go.

Chapter 12

Is Peterson really at war with social justice warriors?

Peterson has attracted the ire of 'social justice warriors'. In its current (pejorative) sense, a social justice warrior is 'a humorless shrill who takes pleasure in demonstrating their superiority by policing the behavior of others' (Massanari and Chess 2018, p. 526; for the origins of this expression, see Ohlheiser 2015). Why the term 'warrior'? Here is one hypothesis, taken from Roger Scruton:

> People reason collectively towards a common goal only in times of emergency—when there is a threat to be vanquished, or a conquest to be achieved. Even then, they need organization, hierarchy and a structure of command if they are to pursue their goal effectively. Nevertheless, a form of collective rationality does emerge in these cases, and its popular name is war. Moreover—and here is the corollary that came home to me with a shock of recognition—any attempt to organize society according to this kind of rationality would involve exactly the same conditions: the declaration of war against some real or imagined enemy. (Scruton 2009, p. 10)

Peterson encourages those who are at war with conservatives not to dismiss half of their country—and the majority of the world—as stupid and/or evil (see his September 2018 conversation with Douglas Murray on *UnHerd*). Yet when it comes to advocates of social justice, he tends to dismiss these (mostly young) people as stupid and/or evil.

There are certainly grounds for doing so. Peterson observes that 'the fervent hope of every undisciplined person (even an undisciplined genius) is that his current worthlessness and stupidity is someone else's fault. If—in the best of cases—it is *society's* fault, then society can be made to pay' (1999, p. 218). This partially explains the rise of identity politics, since '[t]he group steps in—most evidently, at the point of adolescence— and provides "permeable" protective shelter to the child too old for the mother but not old enough to stand alone' (Peterson 1999, p. 222). By contrast, individualism is hard work, since judging seven billion people requires one to render seven billion different judgments. People thus flock to collectivist ideologies in order to flee a society 'where the provision of food and shelter is a responsibility, and not a given; where security —final authority, in the form of parent—no longer exists' (1999, p. 224). Yet despite these perceptive psychological and sociological observations, Peterson rarely entertains the possibility that social justice warriors might be honestly following their own ideals and philosophical reasons.

It may be that embracing social justice is, like wearing a Che Guevara T-shirt, just a fashion statement. However, I submit that if one seriously explores the ideals that drive social justice warriors, one will see that these noisy activists espouse an Other-regarding morality that is wholly consistent with Christian ethics. While Peterson articulates an evolutionary gloss of Biblical texts that supposedly recommends hard-nosed self-reliance, the young people who yearn to defend 'the oppressed' go straight to the core and heed religion's altruistic message of self-sacrifice. It is an unsophisticated and naïve response, to be sure. But, precisely for that reason, it shows the essence of the doctrine.

Peterson's reading of the Bible is idiosyncratic. The Bible's main message is arguably its advocacy of self-sacrificial altruism, not rugged individualism. Although serious scholarly engagements with Peterson's ideas are few and far between, some observers have reached the same conclusion:

> Peterson's second book is filled with reflections on the Biblical narratives concerning Adam and Eve, Cain and Abel, Abraham and Isaac, and the themes of suffering and sacrifice. But when Peterson talks about theological issues, he invariably invokes what Paul Tillich called the vertical or transcendental dimension of faith, the piety of transcendent and inner-worldly concerns. The idea that religious faith must also be lived out in the horizontal dimension, the pursuit of social justice, never seems to cross his mind. [...] Nevertheless, as any serious student of religion knows, the Prophetic call for justice is integral to the Biblical tradition [...]. It is what inspired the Rev. Martin Luther King, Jr. to rally people of conscience to abolish segregation and dis- mantle Jim Crow in the civil rights movement. (Burston 2019, p. 10; see Tillich 1957)

Interestingly, the notion of virtue signalling that critics (like Doidge 2018, p. xx) deploy against social justice warriors was originally developed to explain the evolutionary utility of religious practices. The proposal is that visible practices such as clothing bans, celibacy, blood rituals, and so on persisted throughout human history because they allowed people in a given group to bond. Signalling provides 'a medium in which partners may express and evaluate genuine moral commit- ments' (Bulbulia and Schjoedt 2010, p. 36). However, because of recent technological changes, the costs associated with such outward expressions of virtue have been significantly lowered.

It does not take much, for instance, to righteously 'unfriend' someone on Facebook because of an offensive comment they supposedly made. So instead of providing a means of ascertaining genuine moral commitments, virtue signalling now establishes 'as-if' evidence of moral character. Very few radical feminists, for instance, book one-way tickets to Iran to fight real fights worth fighting (e.g. Siamdoust 2018). It is much easier (and safer) to publish an article in *Hypatia*. So '[w]hile in the past people of rank or status were those and only those who took risks, who had the downside for their actions, [...] today the exact reverse is taking place' (Taleb 2014, p. 6; see also Taleb 2018). The expression 'social justice warrior' is thus aggrandized. Real warriors actually risk their lives.

The lower costs engendered by online social networks have thus changed the explanatory scope of classic signalling theory. Peterson is a sincere person, so he does not like the idea that a person can reap the benefits of public displays of moral conviction without taking any tangible action. Peterson objects to the 'signalling' portion of virtue signalling, but to find a genuine challenge of the 'virtue' portion, one has to look elsewhere.

Consider, for instance, the idea that one should sacrifice oneself for others. Peterson (2018a, p. 263) would no doubt say that if my son is in need, then the right thing for me to do is to provide for him. That would certainly be my choice. Yet what makes my son special? The only plausible answer seems to be that he is *my* son. As a father, I have enveloped him in my value structure, but surely there are other children in this world whose pressing needs far exceed those of my son. Don't these children have a greater claim on my life and/or energy? Here, the difference in ethical rationales starts to matter. According to an Other-regarding morality, I ought to privilege those most in need. By contrast, following a Self-regarding morality, I ought to invest in people whom I value. Peterson clearly does not recommend helping strangers at the expense of one's family.

But importantly, nothing in the Other-regarding morality that he officially endorses licenses such a choice.

There is a tremendous difference between ranking people's needs based on how close those people are to you versus ranking people's needs based on how much need they have. Only the former rank allows you to privilege your child(ren) over others. Now, Peterson is aware that, in a Christian world-view, 'the person who wants to alleviate suffering […] who wants to create Heaven on Earth—will make the greatest of sacrifices, of self and child, of everything that is loved' (2018a, p. 172). The number of people who consider this idea to be an ideal is smaller than the number of people who tangibly act it out. One can presumably wriggle out of this inconsistency or weakness of will by saying that prescriptions about what one 'ought' to do are often too impractical. After all, it is far easier to *talk* about asceticism than to actually follow Jesus's call to leave behind all of one's belongings. However, countering social justice warriors by saying that self-sacrifice is best achieved by mastering self-reliance is not countering self-sacrifice at all. It is disagreeing on a means-to-end fit while leaving the end untouched.

Since none of us truly view the needs of random children to be on par with the needs of our children, and since most people interested in Peterson uncritically accept (or are well acquainted with) the basic tenets of Christianity, Peterson offers a soothing combination. He lets people make sense of the fact that their specific position inevitably confers special status on certain people, events, and projects—without ever challenging their inherited belief that ethically such things should not matter. Peterson thus offers his readers and listeners the guidance of a Self-regarding morality while employing the language of Other-regarding moralities. One symptom of this is that to even state Self-regard, Peterson must make a detour into Other-regard: 'Treat yourself like someone you are responsible for helping' (2018a, p. 31).

Logically, individualism and altruism do not make a stable mixture. But consistency is assessed only by serious scrutiny, and Peterson's ideas rarely receive any. That is too bad, because there are real issues at stake. You will not win against a team that is playing by your accepted rules better than you are. The game 'Tag, you're *forever* it *no matter what*!' was pioneered by Christians. It is called Original Sin. Social justice warriors are daring enough to deploy it in argumentation. However, like a curse, the tactic paralyses only those who accept it.

Peterson is right that social justice warriors employ a simplistic gimmick when they link individuals to groups and then rank groups based on putative degrees of 'oppression' — playing the sceptical card whenever they encounter real objections. Like Peterson, I believe this entire set-up should be abandoned. Still, all this talk about oppression should give one pause. As one critic observed, '[t]wenty years ago, Alan Sokal called postmodernism "fashionable nonsense". Today, post-modernism isn't a fashion — *it's our culture*' (Nathan Cofnas, in Cofnas *et al.* 2018). These trends have attained such rapid cultural prominence precisely because they sing a familiar refrain: you (as a privileged person) are inherently guilty and must repent by giving. Give to whom? We can let the government decide that. Peterson is thus wrong when he says that 'the postmodern, neo-Marxist pastiche that makes up the radical Left philosophy [...] has nothing to do with compassion' (Peterson, in Dyson *et al.* 2018, p. 31). Only compassion can explain why those defined as winners of a socio-economic power struggle would outdo each other in ridding themselves of their winning position.

Let me state this concern as clearly and succinctly as I can. Imagine that there is a 100-metre dash with three lanes and three runners. One runner is fast, one runner is slow, and the third is of medium speed. A race occurs, and each runner runs as fast as their abilities allow. The race is just a brute event in the world — a causal happening without any normative significance. So in order to arrange the participants on a podium, we need to judge the race in light of some general standard. On a 'meritocracy' standard that rewards ability, the fast runner gets the gold medal, the medium runner gets the silver, and the slow runner gets the bronze. On an 'equity' reading that doctors an equality of outcome, all three runners get the same colour of medal (all gold or all silver, say). Now, Peterson is against equity. The starting blocks should be equally aligned, but the performances should reflect the best that each individual musters. Yet how are we to classify the Biblical claim that in the ideal world to be sought, 'The last shall be first and the first last' (Matthew 20:16)? By that standard, the fast runner would get the bronze medal and the slow runner would get the gold. I cannot see how Peterson (2018a, p. 87) can object to equity while at the same time defending an outlook that is even less merit based. Are we witnessing an 'Oppression Olympics' (Ridgway 2012)? Jesus lit the torch.

Of course, religious apologists will no doubt find a way to have their convex and concave podium at the same time. But, to his credit, Jesus spoke plainly. So when one goes against the literal meaning of a prescription, one thereby attests that one is guided by *another* prescription. That's no sin—Jesus's pronouncements are not exempt from the pervasive possibility of error. We can nevertheless get clear on which views are compatible and incompatible.

Participation in organized religion may be on the decline, but religious zeal is not. In March of 2018, Peterson gave a talk at Queen's University where '[t]he 900 or so people who attended (who comported themselves admirably and thoughtfully throughout) were subject [*sic*] to a continual 90-minute barrage of noise generated by the protestors, who leaped up on the stained glass windows lining the hall and banged continually on them, breaking one' (from Peterson's YouTube caption). Why are these people doing this? I want to suggest that most of the protestors view themselves as moral, and that the morality they espouse is, at root, the one found in Christianity.

Peterson never calls into question the idea that there is a utopian 'city of God' and that our cities 'as profanely realized' (1999, p. 14) fall short of it. As he matured from a young socialist (Peterson 2018a, p. 196) to a clinical psychologist, Peterson came to realize that the most effective way to bring about this putative state of harmony is to clean your room (2018a, p. 157). However, the closed fist emblem and slogans that adorn social justice placards capture perfectly Peterson's recommendation to '[s]ay only those things that make you strong' (2018a, p. 158). Likewise, the students who disrupt his public talks are betting that history will view their actions in the same favourable light that we now view the 1960s sit-ins in Birmingham, Alabama. Social justice warriors 'genuinely believe they are in the midst of a civil-rights movement — if a white conservative criticizes them, they wear it as a badge of honor' (Handa 2019). Protesters who oppose Peterson are thus following in earnest Peterson's recommendation to '[d]o only those things that you could speak of with honour' (2018a, p. 158). As for his recommendation to '[l]et your own soul guide you' (2018a, p. 158), anyone who thinks that they are doing the right thing can claim to be following that vague rule.

As 'intersectionality' shows, 'the twin categories of "guilty oppressor" and "justice-seeking victim" can be made endlessly inclusive' (Peterson 2018b, p. xvii). Humans will always invent and sustain new language games that allow them to be on the 'just' side. Humans will destroy others (and flock to their own destruction) so long as their stories tell them that such destruction holds meaning. Peterson 'remembers the great totalitarian threats to human liberty and flourishing that delivered catastrophic levels of death and slavery to those caught in their sway in a relatively short period' (Baker 2020, p. 30). Citing the horrors of collectivist regimes, Peterson asks:

'How much proof do we need?' (2018b, p. xx). Proof of what, exactly? That collectivism does not work, or that it is not a noble ideal? No pile of bodies will ever amount to a proof that collectivism is wrong (and not just impractical). The very idea of an ideal ensures its immunity from falsification.

One could see 'the continued decline of church attendance' (Peterson 2019b) as an indication that commitment to sacrificial altruism is also on the decline. But one could just as easily see it as an indication that commitment to sacrificial altruism has permeated the surrounding culture so fully that it can now stand on its own, without any organized religious support. This explains why, despite flirting with sceptical epistemologies, the 'postmodern' thinkers that Peterson abhors were able to help themselves to the idea of sacrifice. That idea was put in the water and in the air of the West by centuries of Christian thinkers (see, for example, the segment of history recounted by Burke 2010, or the more sweeping account given by Hicks 2004, pp. 180–83).

Peterson's diagnosis of collectivism's dominance is thus correct but incomplete. Consider what he says:

> What happens with the postmodernists is [that] they say: 'Oh, there is an infinite number of interpretations'. And then the human part of you goes: 'Okay… Well, what am I supposed to do *next*, then?' — since there is an infinite number of choices. And the postmodernist says: 'Well, my theory can't account for that'. And then they say: 'Well, back to Marxism!' And so that's why I think there is this unholy alliance between the postmodernists and the new Marxists, because postmodernism is a dead-end from the perspective of applicable wisdom. (Peterson, Joe Rogan podcast number 1006)

Peterson (2018a, pp. 306–11) claims that collectivist politics get snuck in through the back door, but he never addresses why *this* particular political vision gets privileged. After all, the bad line of reasoning astutely identified by Peterson can support any political orientation. One could just as easily take the premise 'There are an infinite number of interpretations' and conclude 'Well, back to Hayek' (given the content of Hayek's views, that particular inference would be more plausible). Peterson is correct that there is an unholy alliance between postmodernism and Marxism, but it has achieved a strong grip on the Western imagination because it gets its moral fuel from an unholy alliance between Marxism and religious altruism (Christian or otherwise).

One's upbringing constrains what one can imagine. So if you distrust grand narratives (Lyotard 1979) but nevertheless want to determine a course of action to take, you do not have to make any overt commitments. Rather, you can let your inter- locutors consult whichever moral code they want and let the limitations of their imagination constrain the possible options. To illustrate, imagine that you are given a menu listing all the types of sandwiches ever made. You are told that, in order to avoid sandwich imperialism, no one will impose on you a preferred sandwich (a Reuben's, say). Now, it is contentious whether postmodernism demands or entails such relativism (see Klein 2018). In any event, the point is that because all the options on the menu contain bread, at a suitable level one can rest assured of the outcome. Similarly, what unites social justice warriors is 'xenophilia' — the love of whatever is other than you *because* it is other than you (Degutis 2006; 2007). The current version of this morality can be traced back to Emmanuel Levinas (2008), but Levinas's appeals to 'the Other' only worked because his audience had already accepted the ideal of self-sacrifice propounded into minds by centuries of religious exhortation.

Students are told by their college and university professors that no system of belief is superior to any other, or at any rate that any claim of superiority is morally problematic (see, for example, Dover 2015). But since all the texts on the students' ethics syllabi agree on a few basics—notably that pursuing one's self-interest is bad (Khawaja 2014)—the outcome is predictable, irrespective of surface variations.

Commenting on the horrors of the Soviet Union, Peterson suggests that 'hate may well be a stronger and more compelling motivator than love' (2018b, p. xv) and sardonically writes: 'How convenient, that the darkest and direst of all possible motivations could be granted the highest of moral standings!' (2018b, p. xvi). By focusing on psychological motivations, Peterson mounts only a surface challenge. He succeeds in showing that our beliefs have an unacknowledged distant source, but he does nothing to establish whether the content of those beliefs is any good. To mount such a challenge is to reject the premise that living in the city of God would be a good thing. Peterson accepts this premise; he only thinks that seeking this ideal state of affairs brings out the worst in people.

We need to be clear on why collectivism is wrong. The problem with collectivist schemes is not that they want people to work together toward a common goal but that they want *everyone* in a society to work together toward a common goal. There are bound to be people who disagree (about the end, the means, or both), so using the governmental apparatus to enforce a given scheme is essentially bypassing the human mind's ability and right to think. Normally, if you want to enlist a person's participation in your project, you must knock at the front door of that individual's mind, offer *reasons*, and accept the possibility that they might refuse. When one embraces collectivism of any sort, this informed consensual procedure—which is the glue of civilized human affairs—gets traded for a muzzle and a club.

Ostensibly, there are do-gooders who feel that their book learning entitles them to dispose of other people's work earnings. A person having to go door to door to convince people of her utopian scheme might get a few to join, but disastrous errors spread on the widest scale when they are enacted into law. Muzzles and clubs don't track truth, so the individual mind is the best bulwark against stupidity and evil.

Peterson expresses puzzlement at the fact that it is 'still acceptable—and in polite company—to profess the philosophy of a Communist or, if not that, to at least admire the work of Marx' (2018b, p. xx). This acceptability is not puzzling: the ideas in question have been accepted. Peterson rejects collectivism, but he does not touch the ethic of self-sacrifice without which that political programme loses its purchase. According to Peterson,

> it is clearly the case that we require a future toward which to orient ourselves—to provide meaning in our life, psychologically speaking. It is for that reason we see the same need expressed collectively, on a much larger scale, in the Judeo-Christian vision of the Promised Land, and the Kingdom of Heaven on Earth. *And it is also clearly the case that sacrifice is necessary to bring that desired end state into being.* (Peterson 2018b, pp. xx–xxi; my emphasis)

Like moths to a flame, humans will always go as far as their unreachable ideals demand. To my mind, 'the longing to restructure the human spirit in the very image of the Communist preconceptions' (Peterson 2018b, p. xix) and the longing to restructure the human spirit in the very image of the Christian preconceptions are both longings to restructure the human spirit.

When we read Peterson carefully and use proven critical thinking tools, we see that there is no valid inference from the premise that pain and suffering are part of the world to the conclusion that '[p]ain and suffering *define* the world' (Peterson 2018a, p. 172; my emphasis). Peterson starts by asking us to recognize the undeniable experience of pain (2018a, p. 35). That is sensible enough. However, he subsequently takes this recognition further than logic licenses.

Emphasizing responsibility is fine, but discussions of responsibility must not lose sight of the fact that delayed gratification (Peterson 2018a, pp. 164–71) is still gratification. Peterson seeks to distance himself from positive psychology's emphasis on happiness (Wong 2011). In Peterson's view: 'It's all very well to think the meaning of life is happiness, but […] what happens when you're unhappy? Then you're a failure' (interviewed in Lott 2018). Again, this is a fallacious inference. It is like saying that if you seek a twenty-pound weight loss and your weight stays flat tomorrow, then you are failure. None of this follows.

On the CBC Radio show *Ideas* hosted by Paul Kennedy, Peterson complains that 'the problem with the public portrayal of the ideal state of humanness as happiness is that it makes all of these young people feel ashamed of their own suffering. They feel that, if they're suffering and if they find their life tragic in its essence that that means there's something wrong with them'. Understanding Peterson charitably, he is saying that stressing the need to be happy can hinder or slow the psychological improvement of unhappy people, because it adds a sense of guilt to the list of challenges that they must overcome. Even though this complaint can have some basis, it is so general that it can be directed at Peterson's preferred compass: meaning. Indeed, one could just as easily say that the problem with Peterson's portrayal of the ideal state as meaningfulness makes young people feel ashamed if they have not found a meaningful path. Hence, one could object that stressing the need to live a meaningful life can hinder or slow the psychological improvement of people who feel that their lives are bereft of meaning, because it adds a sense of guilt to the list of challenges that they must overcome.

On *Ideas*, Peterson reiterated his view that those who think 'that the purpose of life is to be happy […] are idiots'. Far from being idiots, many (most?) serious thinkers on the matter employ the more robust (Aristotelian) concept of flourishing. Part of the problem is that Peterson construes happiness solely as an emotion that vanishes 'like cotton candy' (in Lott 2018). In technical terms, he confuses hedonism and eudaemonism (Delle Fave *et al.* 2010, pp. 4–11). Maybe Peterson knows the difference between happiness and eudaemonia but does not want to get into the niceties of actual philosophical work. This, however, is not a nuance that can be glossed over.

To gauge the difference, consider that since the Olympic Games are held every four years, no human can stand on the winner's podium for more than a few seconds per lifetime. The same can be said of wedding vows. These events do not last much longer than a few orgasms strung together. However, the sense of accomplishment and deep joy that they produce is not 'done in by the first harsh blow that reality deals you' (to quote Peterson's paraphrase of Solzhenitsyn, on *Ideas*). In fact, for a eudaemonist, experiences like these can justify life itself. If Peterson replies that this is what he calls 'meaning', then his beef with the happy idiots reduces to a terminological dispute (that hinges on ignorance of the eudaemonist tradition).

Apart from these flaws, Peterson seems oblivious to the fact that a gloomy worldview that foregrounds suffering invites a host of utopian political schemes. Peterson writes: 'Make that an axiom: to the best of my ability I will act in a manner that leads to the alleviation of unnecessary pain and suffering' (2018a, p. 198). Suffering is not an element, like oxygen, that can increase or reduce in sum and distribution, but rather a first-person qualitative experience that single subjects undergo. So the crucial question that Peterson's 'axiom' leaves untouched is: *whose* suffering? It is one thing to alleviate the suffering of one's own child (as per Peterson 2018a, pp. 341–42, 348–51), but the closet utilitarianism adopted by Peterson ensures that state-based utopian schemes will always win.

One can, if one wishes, view the Earth as a giant hospital, where those who are not born patients are born nurses. There are, however, genuinely different ways to conceive of human existence, both in ethics (e.g. Smith 1998) and in politics (e.g. Rasmussen and Den Uyl 2005). The only way to truly stop the driving engine of social justice movements is to affirm unequivocally that one person's sheer need makes no claim on another person's life and/or energy. Depending on the circumstances, I may want to invest in the needs of someone I value. But taking this course of action because *I value* the person is radically different from taking this course of action because *the other person needs* what I can offer them. Peterson cannot affirm the first rationale in such stark terms—at least so long as the catchphrase 'acting as if God exists' means acting as if the God of Christianity exists. If Peterson did affirm that nobody owes anybody else anything (apart from the social transactions they freely enter into), that would be a game changer.

Peterson says: make the world better and start with your room—the political sphere will eventually fall into place. Social justice warriors say: make the world better and start with the political sphere—your room will eventually fall into place. There is noisy disagreement about the means but silent agreement about the end. It is as if we are all born to be global Scouts and Peterson is merely gathering recruits for the grown-up branch of the movement.

Importantly, neither Peterson nor his opponents ever bother to *argue* for why rational self-interest is evil. In lieu of actual reasons, what we have are overlapping intuitions about the unquestioned nobility of sacrificing one's interests for 'the greater good'. As the Jesuits used to say: give me a child until the age of seven and I will give you the adult (see Brierley 1987). However, beliefs that have dibs on our imagination can be mistaken, so Peterson is frighteningly right when he insists that stories repeatedly told shape us in untold ways.

Chapter 13

Beliefs that have dibs on our imagination can be mistaken

Peterson argues that because what we know and believe has a lineage that predates written history, a tenable theory of knowledge and belief must rest on a theory of myths, rituals, and symbolism (2018a, p. 163). He agrees with Nietzsche that '[w]hat the philosophers called "a rational foundation for morality"' is 'merely a scholarly variation of the common *faith* in the prevalent morality' (Nietzsche 1966, p. 98; see Peterson 1999, p. 78). Yet if Peterson is right that narrative patterns permeate our culture, then all of us hear stories about morality long before we acquire any critical thinking skills. This means that ideas about what counts as praiseworthy or blameworthy enter our stream of consciousness at a time when our ability to evaluate those ideas is almost non-existent.

As we become more adept at distinguishing truth from falsehood, these early beliefs will affect the course of our deliberations. Humans are more prone to rationalizing than to rationality. Hence, candidate ideas that match those we heard as children are regarded as right, whereas ideas that do not match are rejected. Of course, if we knew for certain that the early beliefs we acquired by means of myths and stories were true, this match/mismatch method of assessment would continue to track truths. The problem, however, is that we have no way to tell whether this is the case. Falsehoods and misguided creeds can therefore replicate with as much ease as truths and wise insights.

Peterson calls on the idea of evolutionary pressures to find a way out of this problem. His suggestion is that if a story has been around for a very long time, then we have good grounds to think it is not replete with flat-out falsehoods. This suggestion has some merit, but it is plagued by serious problems.

First, Peterson's evolutionary account runs afoul of nascent belief systems such as young religions. There are many religions that we would today consider questionable — Scientology, say. Yet from a doctrinal standpoint, the things said by L. Ron Hubbard are no wackier than the things said by other prophets. For all we know, Scientology is the belief system that will eventually define humanity. Adherents to that emerging religion are no doubt betting on that. The only difference between Hubbard and an established religious figure like Jesus or Muhammad is the number of years and disciples that each has to their credit. Since, like a Twitter account, the number of followers grows only as the number of years grows, it is too early to tell whether Hubbard's eccentric map of meaning will one day trump the ones now found in other major religions.

The suggestion that being around for a very long time gives a belief a presumption of truth has other bizarre consequences. For instance, by the standards Peterson espouses, a lecture on the New Testament given by Peterson in 100 CE would have lacked a presumption of truth that it supposedly enjoys in 2019 CE. Similarly, if being sixty-seven years removed from Hubbard's teachings is too early to tell whether we should lend credence to those teachings, then sixty-seven years removed from Christ's death would have been too early to tell whether to lend credence to his teachings.

The demand that a belief system expose itself to sufficient evolutionary pressures seems reasonable, but what counts as sufficient evolutionary pressures? What, for example, is the difference between Scientology (founded in 1952 by Hubbard) and Sikhism (founded around 1500 CE by Guru Nanak)? Do we really want to say that Sikhism was subjected to evolutionary pressures while Scientology was not? If so, what sorts of 'pressures'?

The analogy with evolution collapses even further when we try to apply it to stories, especially stories deemed religious. As we saw in Chapter 11, in Peterson's hands, every falsehood or absurdity in the Bible becomes merely an *apparent* falsehood or absurdity. If one insists otherwise, then that just goes to show how shallow one is (see, for example, Peterson's dismissals of Matt Dillahunty). In light of what possible flaw could sacred texts ever be weeded out? Applying the insights of Darwin to the realm of ideas is a promising explanatory strategy (see Popper 1979; Peterson 2018a, p. 194). However, evolutionary pressures are liable to ground religious texts only if there are real pressures — that is, genuine chances of being falsified. Watching Peterson weave *ad hoc* interpretations on his feet, I detect no standard by which his favoured text(s) could ever be shown wrong. If semantic gymnastics ensure that a critically minded person cannot now point to a flaw in the Bible, how could such a person possibly have voiced an objection to the Bible in the early years of that text? The duration of a 'winning streak' no longer matters if the fights of a 'champion' were rigged to win from the start.

In a 2019 debate with Slavoj Žižek, Peterson noted that, while all people think, few people ever consider the possibility that their thinking might be wrong. Opening ourselves to that (admittedly unsettling) possibility, what if established myths and narratives produce only *feelings* of being right? What if, moreover, this feeling of being right is prompted by nothing more than the satisfaction of reconciling disparate fragments of culture? Consider Stephen Beckner's explanation:

> Functioning like a cognitive optical illusion, the trick takes advantage of the brain's tendency to optimize efficiency by constructing models of increasing abstraction. So when ancient tales like Cain and Abel can seem to provide relevant moral lessons in the contemporary world, that new layer of abstraction can *feel* like truth. Sometimes I think an epiphany is simply the brain expressing relief that it has one less rogue data set to account for, one less open file without a drawer to shove it in. It feels good. It feels like your room just got that little bit cleaner, to borrow a metaphor. (Beckner 2018, p. 29)

For the same reasons that experiencing cognitive dissonance is unpleasant, eradicating dissonance is pleasant. Examining one's beliefs thus ruins the fun. Scruton, for instance, questions the benefits of critical thinking. He contends that when we build an evidence-based account, 'we may think ourselves more rational and better equipped for life in the modern world. But in fact we are less well equipped, and our new beliefs are far less justified, for the very reason that they are justified by ourselves' (Scruton 2009, p. 12). This recommendation to eschew the examination of strongly held convictions may sound noble when what one has in mind are benign ideals of polite civility. However, jihadists could just as easily revel in this idea that their beliefs are especially important by virtue of being unjustified and unjustifiable.

Historically, a prominent repudiation of reason and evidence in favour of faith was articulated by Al-Ghazali in his eleventh-century book *Tahafut al-Falasifa* (*The Incoherence of the Philosophers*, 1963), which has influenced a large segment of the world population ever since. The polymath Averroes wrote a reply piece titled *Tahafut al-Tahafut* (*The Incoherence of the Incoherence*, 1987), but it had little discernible effect.

In any event, when Scruton joins Al-Ghazali to repudiate 'the abstract rational systems of the philosophers' (Scruton 2009, p. 12), he paints with too broad a brush. Not everybody in the history of philosophy believes that rigorous thought must swipe away everything and start from scratch. Peirce, for example, held that '[w]e must begin with all the prejudices which we actually have when we enter upon the study of philosophy. These prejudices are not to be dispelled by a maxim, for they are things which it does not occur to us *can* be questioned' (1931–58, vol. 5, para. 265). While Peirce recognized that 'we cling tenaciously, not merely to believing, but to believing just what we do believe' (vol. 5, para. 372), he was adamant that dogmatism, 'which may be called the method of tenacity, will be unable to hold its ground in practice' (vol. 5, para. 378). You simply cannot hide from the truth. Sooner or later, your errors will make a practical difference.

This does not mean that human reason can put everything into words. After all, if one goes through the trouble of taking a flat-Earther into space and asks that sceptic to look out the window, it is expected that the verdict rendered by such an experience will be decisive (Champagne 2016d). If, upon viewing our spherical planet from space, our interlocutor continues to maintain that the Earth is flat, we are fully within our rational rights to dismiss that interlocutor and halt our efforts at persuasion. In this sense, the scientific method comprises moments of mandatory silence. Such silence, however, is not mysticism, so appeals to evidence remain the final arbiters of true or false claims. By contrast, when we rely on the strengths of our convictions as our compass, we do not give ourselves any means of ascertaining whether our beliefs are pointing in the right direction. Psychological premises cannot yield epistemological conclusions. To ascertain matters pertaining to knowledge, we need to pool our best arguments and evidence. Only then can we credit our beliefs with being true (Champagne 2015a).

The problem, as Peterson points out, is that we only start pondering the meaning of life *after* we have inherited a more or less cohesive answer to that question. Since children get their first moral guidance from their parents or guardians, Piaget conjectured that early memories of parental authority provide a 'theory of the filial origin of the religious sense' (2013, p. 88). Piaget held that 'the respect felt by the small for the great plays an essential part' in explaining 'what makes the child accept all the commands transmitted to him by his parents' (2013, p. 102). Mature minds can entertain the largest being of all, God. This may explain why a religious person requires a person-like entity to forbid and permit their actions. The Christian tradition, for instance, openly refers to God as the Father.

Our parents or guardians thus have an outsized influence on our thinking. This has to be the starting point of our reflection. After all, like all human beings, I was 'thrown' into the world. But, while I was born a Catholic, I do not have to die one, so in the intervening years I am free to *think*. Reality —'that which selects'— has given me good reasons to change my mind (i.e. drop bad ideas and adopt better ones).

Peterson was also raised a Christian. At the age of thirteen, he was introduced to the writings of Ayn Rand. In the same year that Peterson earned his PhD, the United States Library of Congress and the Book of the Month Club commissioned a survey that resulted in Rand's *Atlas Shrugged* being ranked the second-most influential book, after the Bible (see Fein 1991). Since Rand advocates rationality-based self-interest instead of faith-based self-sacrifice, Peterson's encounter with her work must have caused cognitive dissonance. Such dissonance can be dealt with in one of three ways (Festinger 1957, p. 264):

1. By changing one or more of the elements involved in dissonant relations.

2. By adding new cognitive elements that are consonant with already existing cognition.
3. By decreasing the importance of the elements involved in the dissonant relations.

We have some leeway on how to achieve a coherent set of beliefs. Taking path (2), Peterson rescued his belief in the Bible by essentially turning Jesus into a Randian hero.

Truth be told, Rand pre-chewed Peterson's reconciliation. Comparisons have been made between the strikers of *Atlas Shrugged* and Talmudic myths (Merrill 1991, pp. 61–62). In terms of Christian imagery, the main hero of *Atlas*, John Galt, ends up tortured by his enemies, who strap him naked in crucifix-like fashion with 'small metal disks of electrodes at the ends of the wires [...] attached to his wrists, his shoulders, his hips and his ankles' (Rand 1957, p. 1043). According to the archivist Jeffrey Britting, Rand 'spent hours contemplating [Salvador Dali's painting *Corpus Hypercubus*] at the Metropolitan Museum of art', and she 'even felt a kinship between her personal view of John Galt's defiance over his torture in *Atlas Shrugged* and Dali's depiction of the suffering of Jesus' (2004, p. 93). Peterson is also gripped by crucifixion imagery (see the anecdote in *Maps of Meaning*, p. xix). In any event, at one point during Galt's torture session, the engine providing the electric charges breaks down. No one knows how to fix it. No one, that is, except Galt, who in the 'competent tone of an engineer' proceeds to explain to his torturers how to mend the broken wires. This literary metaphor is meant to illustrate that without support from the good, evil is too impotent to win. So if one withdraws one's support, evil stands a greater chance of being defeated.

Rand called this the 'sanction of the victim' thesis. Tibor Machan explains the thesis as follows:

> Suppose you need to go to a neighborhood where car thefts are frequent and yours is a desirable model. Instead of

locking up your vehicle good and hard, you leave the doors unlocked and the key in the ignition. It is, as most reasonably expected, stolen. Those who stole it aren't morally innocent, but neither are you. They perpetrated theft, you failed to be prudent. Now consider all the millions of people who are victimized by statists throughout history and throughout the contemporary world. [...] Both those who sanction the statism and those who would resist it are victims since statism is wrong in and of itself [...]. But *refusal to acknowledge that the statism is morally wrong is itself morally wrong, as is the refusal to take measures to fend it off.* (Machan 2007, p. 78; my emphasis)

While the presence or absence of a wrongdoing is largely (and sometimes completely) out of one's control, one's actions can aid or hinder that wrongdoing—and those actions are very much under one's control. Acting in accordance with one's conscience is the virtue of integrity (Smith 2006, pp. 176–97). Compare this Randian stance with what Peterson has to say:

Nothing brings a better world into being than the stated truth. Now, you might have to pay a price for that. But, that's fine—you're going to pay a price for every bloody thing you do and everything you don't do. You don't get to choose to not pay a price. You get to choose which poison you're going to take. That's it. So, if you are going to stand up to something, stand up for your truth. [...] It is not safe to speak, and it never will be. But, the thing you have to keep in mind is that *it is even less safe not to speak.* [...] The truth is what redeems the world from hell [...] and we saw plenty of hell over the last hundred years. (Peterson, February 2017 talk at the Manning Centre Conference)

Like Peterson, Rand held that such moral insights are best conveyed in a narrative format. Peterson thinks that Rand 'was actually more powerful as a fiction writer than as a philosopher. And that's not a denigrating comment, because I don't believe that philosophy is a higher calling than fiction. [...] I enjoyed reading *Atlas Shrugged*' (discussion with Dave Rubin, November 2017). Despite this praise, Peterson does not think 'her take on things was sufficiently differentiated and sophisticated', since according to him 'she doesn't place the struggle between good and evil *inside* her characters, it's always *between* her characters—and that's a mistake'. Peterson is essentially faulting Rand for not following Solzhenitsyn's claim that 'the line dividing good and evil cuts through the heart of every human being' (Solzhenitsyn 2018, p. 75). Does this criticism have any textual basis?

It is poetic justice that Rand, who frequently dismissed thinkers without reading them carefully, is now being dismissed without being read carefully. If one looks solely at the bookends of the good and evil spectrum, like the characters John Galt (good) and Ellsworth Toohey (evil), Peterson's criticism seems to hold. By design, Rand made sure that 'her noble people are too noble and her ignoble people are too ignoble' (Peterson, talking to Rubin). But for Peterson's criticism to apply it must overlook many other characters who fall somewhere between these two extremes. For instance, Rand explicitly placed the characters of *The Fountainhead* on a spectrum, precisely to illustrate—in archetypal form—the range of existential possibilities that result from human choices: 'Howard Roark: the man who can be and is. Gail Wynand: the man who could have been. Peter Keating: the man who never could be and doesn't know it. Ellsworth M. Toohey: the man who never could be—and knows it' (Rand, in Harriman 1999, p. 93). Similarly, in *Atlas*, the character Hank Rearden is an industrialist whose 'words and deeds initially sanction an unearned guilt' for his productiveness and who initially 'viewed his passion for Dagny as animalistic and degrading' (Younkins 2014, p. 139). Peterson completely overlooks the way in which Rand's novel follows Rearden's inner struggle. This oversight is problematic, given that Rearden is essentially a Petersonian hero who starts off flawed yet gradually overcomes obstacles to reach health 'both in economics and business and in romantic and other human relationships' (Younkins 2014, p. 139).

Even if one agrees with Solzhenitsyn and Peterson that all humans house both good and bad within them, it is unclear why this fact should be reflected in fiction as well. We don't turn to art forms like literature for a journalistic report of how humans are, but rather for an idealization of how humans could and should be. In any event, Rand's first novel, *We the Living*, set in Soviet Russia, offers the reader plenty of Peterson-style suffering.

If you made it out of a gulag alive, what world would you like to live in? In times of hardship and confusion, literary idealizations can offer both spiritual and political guidance. At one point, Rand's hero Galt is forced on television to kowtow to buzzwords such as 'unity' and 'the people's cause'. Far from being a supporter of this, Galt faces the cameras and proclaims, 'Get the hell out of my way!' (Rand 1957, p. 1030). Rand was essentially illustrating Solzhenitsyn's dictum: 'The simple act of an ordinary brave man is not to participate in lies, not to support false actions! His rule: Let *that* come into the world, let it even reign supreme—only not through me' (quoted in Peterson 2018b, p. xii).

Peterson displayed similar defiance when he appeared on *The Agenda* to voice his concerns about compelled speech. Peterson's worries have since been vindicated (see, for example, Hopper 2017; as well as Murphy 2019), but he was initially deemed alarmist. Hence, when Peterson first expressed his dissent, he was in danger of losing his academic position. Ostensibly, these risks did not diminish his resolve—quite the opposite; Peterson had a Galt-like moment when, in front of countless television viewers, he proclaimed: 'I'm not doing this—and that's that'.

Like any human behaviour, Peterson's resolve admits of multiple interpretations. We might say that its main source of inspiration was the Christian myth of the crucifixion, which stresses Christ's 'full participation in and freely chosen acceptance of his fate' (Peterson 1999, p. 452). Yet one could just as easily say that Peterson was acting out a scene from *Atlas Shrugged* which he had read as a boy.

Although more scholarship is needed, the foregoing should suffice to establish that Peterson's ideas mix Randian and Christian motifs (for more parallels, see Kotter 2012). From a psychological standpoint, it is understandable that Peterson should try to reconcile beliefs that, when jointly considered, lead to cognitive dissonance. Peterson writes about young people who, early in their life, 'define their utopia and then bend their lives into knots trying to make it a reality' (2018a, p. 210). The late Christopher Hitchens likewise marvelled at 'how much contortion is required, to receive every new insight of science and manipulate it so as to "fit" with the revealed words of ancient man-made deities' (2007, p. 7). These descriptions capture well Peterson's attempt to reconcile individualism and Christianity. Christianity no doubt entered Peterson's stream of consciousness first, but the Bible does not contain any televised broadcasts.

Peterson's blend of the two most influential books in the United States is untenable, but it has triggered a productive conversation. While Peterson credits mainly the Christian side of this mix with buttressing his outspoken individualist stance, it is unclear whether this self-description is accurate. That is too bad, because some of the secular elements in Peterson's thinking contain exactly the kind of narrative guidance and inspiration that Peterson and his followers are looking for—without the supernatural and dogmatic baggage.

Chapter 14

The story is not over

I prefaced this book by saying that Peterson is involved in one of the great debates of our age. In the tenth chapter, I summarized Peterson's stance by distinguishing between an ethic of divinity, an ethic of community, and an ethic of autonomy (see Shweder *et al.* 1997). Each of these ethical systems places objects and events in a hierarchy. Jonathan Haidt, an ally of Peterson when it comes to free speech, is correct that 'as soon as you step outside of Western secular society', the individual ceases to be the central unit of concern, being replaced with 'larger entities such as families, teams, armies, companies, tribes, and nations' (2012, p. 116) — as well as the largest entity possible, God. But since the verdicts rendered by different ethical systems are bound to differ in non-trivial ways, *we have to place humanity's major hierarchies in a hierarchy*. This is the great debate of our age.

Haidt sets 'aside the question of whether any of these alternative moralities are *really* good, true, or justifiable' (2012, p. 114). He thinks humans are not rational enough to consider this issue in a level-headed manner. He may well be right. Yet, as Yaron Brook put it in a July 2018 conversation with Peterson, 'there is no way for us to have different foundations and not come up with different conclusions'. To make this concrete, if a person on the verge of detonating a nuclear bomb in a major city believes that they are fulfilling 'God's will', their ethic of divinity will no longer be a matter of personal preference.

Similarly, the day the ethic of community leads governments to adopt an income tax system graduated according to alleged degrees of 'group privilege', a sleeping giant will awaken with terrible resolve.

Actions taken upon waking are usually not the most rational. So even though 'we are dividing, and polarizing, and drifting toward chaos' (Peterson 2018a, p. 361), it would be nice to engage in some thinking, while we still can. Spearheading this conversation, Peterson argues that the ethic of autonomy should be placed above the ethic of community. As he writes: 'Every person is unique—and not just in a trivial manner: importantly, significantly, meaningfully unique. Group membership cannot capture that variability. Period' (2018a, p. 316). I agree. However, if we pit the ethic of autonomy against the ethic of divinity and ask which is on top, Peterson waffles. I, on the other hand, want to be crystal clear: for the reasons laid out in this book, I rank the ethic of autonomy above its competitors, divinity included.

As we saw in Chapter 11 when we discussed the word 'meek', if you turn to the Bible or some other revered text for guidance, *you* are in charge of what passages you emphasize, what passages you conveniently overlook, what interpretive spins you give, etc. In fact, since your place of birth does not force you to adopt the religion(s) around you, you are the one who picks the text on which you perform these various interpretations. No one—not Jesus, not your parents, not Peterson, not some cleric—will spare you from judging philosophical matters on your own. Norman Doidge, in his foreword to *12 Rules for Life*, is thus clearer than Peterson: 'the foremost rule is that you must take responsibility for your own life. Period' (Doidge 2018, p. xxiii).

When it comes to collectivism, Peterson can be 'seen as a man who spies a glowing ember remaining in an otherwise extinguished fire. Unless it is put out, the ember may flare up into an inferno that once again engulfs its surroundings' (Baker

2020, p. 32). However, religion has its own glowing embers. Is it really a 'model of the honourable man' when one 'offers up his life for the advancement of Being—who allows God's will to become manifest fully within the confines of a single, mortal life' (Peterson 2018a, p. 171)? Peterson clearly has some benevolent image in mind when he writes this, but I could easily see the 9/11 hijackers reciting that view.

Of course, such readings tend to be dismissed by the devout as bad faith readings. Sacred texts, on this view, are more complex than their simplistic appearances let on. As a result, when ideas are couched in religious language, every criticism can be charged with missing the target (for more on this fallacious motif, see Law 2018). I agree that the 'interpretation of a given symbol [is] difficult—particularly when it has been removed from its culturally-constructed surroundings or milieu' (Peterson 1999, p. 104). I also agree with Peterson that, most of the time, we acquire our value systems implicitly, via the exemplary actions of characters in narratives. However, 'those committed to the mythic way of knowing inevitably […] have to ask whose interpretations are the best and wisest. Are all myths equally valid, and are interpretations of those myths equally valid?' (Dart 2020, pp. 76–77).

As sectarian divisions and religious wars show, even when people agree on the texts that they consider sacred, those texts can mean many things to many people. This ought to make such sources harmless. What is problematic, however, is that religion is one of the few domains of human discourse where believing something without evidence is regarded as a good thing. So to gain an immediate sense of stability in an uncertain world, one need only follow the no-fail recipe identified by Harris (2007):

1. First, you must want to believe in God.
2. Next, understand that believing in God in the absence of evidence is especially noble.

3. Then, realize that the human ability to believe in God in the absence of evidence might itself constitute evidence for the existence of God.
4. Now consider any need for further evidence (both in yourself and in others) to be a form of temptation, spiritually unhealthy, or a corruption of the intellect.
5. Refer to steps 2–4 as acts of 'faith'.
6. Return to 2.

Peterson ostensibly wants to believe in God. Yet in contrast with step 2, he intends his account to be evidence-based. Peterson claims, for instance, that monotheistic belief is a low resolution pattern capturing the human predicament across all places and times. I am sympathetic to such a wide-scale inquiry (and have even made suggestions for how it might be rigorously conducted; see Champagne 2016a). Yet by framing his account in historical terms, Peterson has exposed himself to the possibility of empirical refutation. If, for example, some scholar of Sumerian culture were to uncover hard evidence that these ancient people did not construe the world in the manner that Peterson (1999, p. 118) claims they did, this evidence would (partly) undermine Peterson's overall proposal.

The problem, as I see it, is that there are two bodies of data and two explanations, yet Peterson gives us only one of each. The first body of data comprises every document and artefact that Peterson incorporates in *Maps of Meaning*. Even if we take for granted that Peterson at least tries to show how stories from disparate cultures exhibit common patterns, this does nothing to address the other explanation needed—namely, why the cultural items absent from Peterson's work were omitted. We might call these omitted items the second body of data. Despite Peterson's encyclopaedic aspirations, this absent body is arguably much larger than anything found in his writings. Yet if one is going to make claims that range over all of humanity, one must either limit oneself to *a priori* logical arguments or engage in *a posteriori* scholarship that ranges over all of humanity. Peterson clearly favours an *a posteriori* route, but this approach is vulnerable to any attack that makes use of the many examples he never mentions.

For instance, if monotheistic religious conceptions are indeed arrived at by a Darwinian battle royal between gods with restricted powers, then polytheistic systems should eventually be wiped out. Clearly, the continued existence of examples such as Hinduism show that this prediction does not bear out. Second, if monotheistic conceptions truly united opposites, we would expect God to be described as 'It', not 'Him'. Again, this prediction does not bear out. Third, as Peterson himself acknowledged (in a conversation with Sam Harris and Douglas Murray on July 16, 2018), '[t]here are Christian substructures' like 'the Russian Orthodox Church, where the same metaphysical principles apply but out of which a democracy did not emerge'. Hence, Peterson's account of the historical origins and political consequences of monotheism is falsifiable (Popper 2002, pp. 43–78) and false. Even on purely logical grounds, there are good reasons to doubt that mono-theism is the terminus of all consistent theological reflection (see Champagne 2020). One should thus be mindful that Peterson's account is persuasive only as long as one cherry picks facts that fit the desired narrative.

From a methodological standpoint, mentioning facts that don't fit is as important as mentioning facts that fit. As the British journalist Helen Lewis said in a 2018 exchange with Peterson for *GQ* magazine: 'I think you're anthropomorphizing [lobsters] to a ridiculous degree. These are creatures that urinate out of their faces.' It is one thing to claim that the New Testament's emphasis on the individual was an improvement over the Old Testament's emphasis on the tribe, but as Peterson's friend Ben Shapiro reminded him (in a discussion on *The Rubin Report*), there are important religions (notably Judaism) that stop with the Old Testament and do not let go of the tribe and do not consider Christ a saviour. Or, to pick a far more devastating case, I am not convinced that if one takes the Quran as one's textual input, one gets freedom and individualism as one's political output.

Peterson has acknowledged that some major world religions do not fit neatly in his story (see his comments in Cseko 2018). Hence, I wonder whether he needs to frame his ideas in historical terms — let alone such broad historical terms. One could just as easily drop all pretensions of historical accuracy and say that one's interpretation of past human stories is *useful*. For a pragmatist, that should be plenty. Peterson's appeal to human history thus strikes me as a rhetorical device, aimed mainly at giving his worldview a certain pedigree. What would we do, for instance, if it were shown beyond all reasonable doubt that most of our forebears intended humankind to jump into a giant volcano? If what my predecessors said or believed hinders my flourishing, then I don't care what they said or believed. It thus seems to me that Peterson could and should justify his proposals on independent grounds, without additionally claiming that his views are the culmination of some long-simmering cross-cultural reflection.

Nietzsche said that every philosophy is 'the personal confession of its author and a kind of involuntary and unconscious memoir' (1966, p. 13). Speaking with Dennis Prager in May 2019, Peterson stated that Christianity (specifically Catholicism) is 'as sane as people can get'. It is quite a coincidence that amid all the belief systems in human history, the one that Peterson was exposed to turns out to be the best. In Chapter 8, we looked at the human propensity to universalize moral assessments by thinking that what holds for me holds for everyone. This inference seems innocuous, but it can have disastrous consequences. To see this, consider the following game. Players are scattered on a playing field marked by a grid. Everyone starts on a different square of that grid. The rules are simple:

the grid one is standing on at the beginning of the game is the goal, so points are accumulated every time an additional person is dragged onto one's initial grid square. What would such a game look like in practice? Clearly, because no one shares the same point of departure, this is as close as we can come to a recipe for a war of all against all. Hence, few people would regard this as a game worth playing. Yet in real life, most people spend a lot of time and energy doing basically just that.

One starts one's life at a specific spot on the globe. This place of birth pretty much settles what religion, if any, one will follow. There is no causal link, but if all I know about an individual is that she was born, say, in Morocco, betting that she is a Buddhist would not be the safest bet. Now, if there is one teaching that all religions have in common, it is that the religion in question is to be preferred. No creed enjoins its believers to believe in another creed. Not everyone is required to proselytize, or to proselytize with the same degree of militancy. Even so, it seems fair to say that, all other things being equal, a Muslim would prefer the whole world to be Muslim, a Christian would prefer the whole world to be Christian, and so on. At the root of this is an aesthetic yearning to make the world uniform. Yet since geography is the best predictor of religious affiliation, and since place of birth necessarily varies, a modicum of game theory and historical knowledge will show that a peaceful outcome is essentially precluded by the initial conditions. The ethic of divinity thus gives rise to a game that cannot be iterated without descending into group conflict.

Peterson says that ethics studies right and wrong, whereas '[r]eligion concerns itself […] with good and evil themselves — with the archetypes of right and wrong' (2018a, p. 102). Calling one's preferred vision 'religious' does not elevate that vision to a higher status, any more than adding an exclamation mark after a claim justifies that claim. A religious idea is simply an idea that one is not willing to give up, no matter how high the pile of evidence against it. When it comes to collectivist schemes, Peterson has come to the conclusion that the pile of corpses is high enough to abandon the whole idea. He is right that the collectivist atrocities of the twentieth century are wrong. However, one can robustly denounce the use of force in human affairs without making a tenuous detour into comparative religious studies, neuroscience, and prehistory.

The observations made at the start of Chapter 10 can be the fulcrum of a more direct stance: I exist in a world, I am capable of knowing that world, I am responsible for my projects/judgments, and I expect others to treat me as a being fitting that description—that is, as a being whose life matters and whose mind must be appealed to, not forced (Champagne 2011b). Peterson gave us a shining example of such a defence when he publicly stood by his judgment on *The Agenda* with Steve Paikin. Now, like any way of life, such an individualist ethos needs its own myths, symbols, and rituals. However, one does not have to find some historical precedent in order to look up to a hero now. In fact, one could argue that this independence from history is precisely why heroes are such potent ethical devices. My oldest son did not have to learn much to admire and emulate Marvel's cinematic heroes—and neither did the viewers gauging Peterson's sincerity and resolve on television.

Peterson would likely object that these heroic behaviours have a psychological hold on our imagination because they are archetypal. His various glosses of ancient tales, novels, and popular movies are intended to show that since archetypes are large-scale patterns that govern our most basic categories, and since these patterns are grounded in the past, a full study of the psyche must involve a study of the past. Acknowledging the motivational powers of archetypes without acknowledging their evolutionary lineage would therefore be disingenuous, or at any rate misguided. Following the methodology advocated by Jung, Peterson would instead insist that to make sense of a child's fascination with superheroes, '[i]t is absolutely necessary to supply these fantastic images [...] with some kind of context so as to make them more intelligible' and that 'the best way to do this is by means of comparative mythological material' (Jung 1968, p. 33). Or, in the argot of Peterson: 'Narrative description of archetypal behavioral patterns and representational schemas — *myth* — appears as an essential precondition for social construction and subsequent regulation of complexly civilized individual presumption, action and desire' (1999, p. 78). I cannot underscore enough how much I agree with this. My disagreement with Peterson is that while the historical repository of stories that shape each person is a necessary *starting point* of one's deliberation, it should not set the end point of those deliberations.

If Peterson is right that the gods of polytheism can 'die' (i.e. lose their cultural/intellectual plausibility in a battle of ideas), then so can the God of monotheism. Peterson, as we saw, accepts that '[t]he "death of God" in the modern world looks like an accomplished fact' (1999, p. 245). Now, the death of God is a traumatic event, if anything is (Peterson 2018a, p. 188; Lavrin 1969, p. 162). However, a truly antifragile individual should emerge stronger from such a trauma.

Rehabilitating age-old narratives should definitely be part of the recovery process. After all, if a given story or symbolism works fine as a motivator, why change it? Moreover, '[a]sking people to give up all forms of sacralized belonging and live in a world of purely "rational" beliefs might be like asking people to give up the Earth and live in colonies orbiting the moon' (Haidt 2012, p. 307). The influential human-made documents at the core of world religions will not and should not be forgotten. With that in mind, 'Peterson has chosen to retell ancient tales as myth in order to reclaim, in some ways, virtue ethics and the older understanding of the formation of character' (Dart 2020, pp. 71–72). That is a worthwhile contribution. There are, however, three tenses to consider — past, present, future — so an account of our shared past (if indeed it is shared) can only be partial.

Here, moving forward, is what must be done. The first order of business is to adopt better concepts. In discussions of religious belief, it is customary to distinguish between 'theism' (according to which a personal God judges our actions, listens to our prayers, orchestrates occasional miracles, takes sides in our conflicts, etc.) and a weaker 'deism' (according to which God set the world in motion but then sat back to watch his creation unfold according to predictable laws). Atheism, then, is defined negatively, as the rejection of theism. Yet if believers in God get to specify what *kind* of God they intend, why shouldn't disbelievers in God also get to specify what *kind* of Godless world they intend? As the *Stanford Encyclopedia of Philosophy* reports, 'many writers at least implicitly identify atheism with a positive metaphysical theory like naturalism or even materialism' (Draper 2017). Peterson routinely makes that identification (in the same way that he routinely identifies the pursuit of happiness with short-range hedonism). However, what are we to make of thinkers, such as myself, who reject God yet also reject materialism and naturalism? I don't want to be clumped with those who endorse a world without (enough) meaning. One way to put such a worldview at arm's length is to insist that disbelief in God comes in two varieties: dis-enchanted atheism and enchanted atheism (using adjectives proposed by Max Weber; see Jenkins 2000). I endorse only the latter.

One could also call this 'meaning-full atheism'. I am less interested in the label than in the idea it is trying to pick out (when a philosophy gets widely adopted, it sheds its -ism any-way and simply gets called common sense). At the moment, the stance I am gesturing at is the most underdeveloped piece of conceptual real estate in philosophy of religion. Recognizing this, our goal should not be to undermine the power that traditional religions have on our imaginations but rather to outdo that power by crafting something even more attractive. Indeed, 'systems are more vulnerable to ennui than to disproof. They are citadels, much shot at perhaps, but never taken by storm, which are quietly discovered one day to be no longer inhabited. The way in which an influential philosopher may undermine the empire of his predecessors consists, one may say, chiefly in his providing his contemporaries with other interests' (Warnock 1958, p. 11).

Achieving this shift requires (among other things) a viable theory of values, a viable theory of consciousness, a viable theory of meaning, and a viable theory of aesthetic experience and ritual. Peterson has contributed to such theories, but the take-away lesson of my evaluation section is that we can and should develop our accounts without taking on the irrational contradictions of supernatural posits and infallible texts.

Manifestly, it is easier to affirm that God is not real than to figure out what to do next. Demolition jobs, no matter how brilliantly executed (e.g. Harris 2008), won't do. Failure to produce a viable ethical, cultural, and political programme is arguably the main weakness of the New Atheists. Harris tries to build an ethical framework, but his wilful disregard of professional work in ethics (Harris 2010, p. 197 n. 1; p. 207 n. 12) leads him to reinvent utilitarianism—in a version completely unresponsive to the criticisms that this view underwent in actual debates (e.g. Smart and Williams 1973, pp. 75–150). As a result of 'cultivating a willed ignorance of the history of ideas, [Harris] is able to avoid noticing that atheism and illiberalism have often been bedfellows. He can then pass over the fact' — hammered home with great force by Peterson—'that the liberal values he claims to profess originated in monotheism' (Gray 2018, p. 22). We need new New Atheists.

Imaginations can change over time. My children will certainly see things differently. So tell a better story and people will gather around it—in the long run, at least (this qualification is crucial). I have added technical bricks to the value and consciousness buildings (see my 2011a, 2015c, and 2018a, respectively). This constructive endeavour is attracting workers from different intellectual backgrounds. One could point to the various 'manifestos' of humanist associations. Yet if the problem with religious texts is that they will never come out as revised editions, the problem with humanist tracts is that they are constantly being revised. Since these would-be movements illustrate Peterson's (2018a, p. 193) observation that we cannot invent our own values without paying heed to what came before, their cultural influence has been close to nil. In response, some atheists have started mimicking the tactics of identity politics and evangelical discourse (Cimino and Smith 2007). This is misguided. One should not have to 'sell' a better alternative. If it is indeed better, a majority of minds will adopt it, in the same way that DVDs completely replaced VHS tapes — without any 'DVD advocacy' or 'VHS debunking'.

The merit of a view is not gauged by the number of people it attracts. Adopting a better philosophy yields immediate dividends in one's lifetime, in the same way that early adopters of DVDs enjoyed the practical benefits right away, irrespective of the coming sea change in consumer habits. The question of whether a secular yet enchanted outlook will ever become part of mainstream culture is thus for future generations to determine. Peterson is impressed, quite rightly, by how far back humanity's timeline extends. Yet that line also extends as far (or further?) into the future, so we would do well to take 'into account the neglected evolutionary future of life on our planet — a possibly billion-year-long future that, whether it eventually passes humans by or not, may eventually see intelligent beings on Earth much better equipped to adjudicate religious issues than we are' (Schellenberg 2013, p. 146). Nothing in the concept of truth requires it to surface fully in one generation, let alone in one's own generation. In keeping with the fourth claim identified in the summary, the individual *is* divine — we just don't know how to say that without sounding weird. For now.

None of this is inexorable, however. We therefore need to be clear on what we did right. Let us suppose that Peterson is correct that individualism has its roots, not in the European Enlightenment, but in the much older Judeo-Christian tradition. As far as I am concerned, this longer history is cause to rejoice. However, to say that individualism originated in the Judeo-Christian tradition does not entail that the view is best defended within that tradition. After all, we do not think that because Peterson was born in rural Alberta his life is best spent in rural Alberta. While building on tradition is inevitable and indeed desirable, Peterson's individualist project is ultimately hindered by the non-revisable character and self-sacrificial content of religious belief.

Why should we assume that an idea found in the past is wiser simply because it is in the past? A prescription such as 'Conserve the social/political/cultural orders that are already in place, since they have likely proven their worth' looks attractive, but on further examination it offers little practical guidance.

For example, take one of the major issues on the desk of any serious European politician at the time of writing: Brexit. A respectable conservative position, probably the majority position, is that the rule of the European Commission (the 'Belgian Empire', as one prominent conservative thinker referred to it in a conversation with me) is alien to the norms of British governance in its methods, its principles and its aims. [...] Nonetheless, another respectable conservative position is that stability is vital not only for business and the economy, but also for citizens' navigation through an increasingly complex social environment. [...] Relations may be tense at the national level, but when it comes to, say, policing organised crime, there is no substitute for the relevant senior police officers from across the continent sitting together around a table, fully confident of a legal framework in which they can share data, request arrests and extradition, and plan cross-border surveillance. 45 years in the life of a nation, even one as venerable as the United Kingdom, is not nothing. [...] It seems reasonable to say that a conservative could go either way on Brexit consistent with his conservatism. (O'Hara 2019, p. 46)

Although there is some truth to the observation that '[m]uch of the ideological conflict over change versus the status quo [...] pertains to age-old disputes concerning the proper role of hierarchy, authority, and inequality' (Jost *et al.* 2009, p. 310), this observation will not take us very far, since it leaves unanswered *what kind of* hierarchy, *what kind of* authority, and *what kind of* inequality we are talking about. Labels such as 'conservative' and 'liberal' do not specify this. Even so, when those labels hit the ear drums of their respective partisans, they each prompt a distinct mental image. Alas, vagueness and confidence are never a good mix.

One would have thought that, given his insistence on precision in language, Peterson (2018a, pp. 259–83) would have been the first to drop facile labels that mean different things to different people. When it comes to forced gender pronouns—the issue that propelled him to fame—Peterson is adamant that one should not employ terms crafted by one's intellectual opponents. Following this principle, I have been able to intelligibly articulate my claims in this book without resorting to isms such as 'liberalism' and 'conservatism'. Voting (in a given election cycle) is something you *do*, not something you *are*. There is no phenomenology inherent to being a 'leftist' or 'rightist'. In fact, people made sense of the world and political affairs quite well—and quite differently—before this contingent dichotomy from revolutionary France got disseminated by Marxists (and, later, television newscasters). As Crispin Sartwell points out, political thinkers such as Henry David Thoreau 'articulated perfectly coherent positions that cannot possibly be characterized as on the left or the right' (Sartwell 2014). If one cannot envision what such alternative positions look like, then that just goes to show how badly one needs to update one's map of meaning.

In religion and in politics, it takes an antifragile mind to actually consider criticisms and revise one's beliefs accordingly. To its credit, the Christian tradition (especially via scholastic logic and dialectics) is in part responsible 'for the emergence of the disciplined but free modern mind' (Peterson 2018a, p. 191) capable of doing this. Some cultures and traditions, by contrast, fail to display the minimal conditions required for critical reflection. As we saw in Chapter 13, by couching his ideas in a familiar Christian language, Peterson offers his readers and listeners individualism with training wheels. The popularity of this intermediary account shows how badly it is needed. Yet because there are situations where the ethics of autonomy, community, and divinity cannot peacefully coexist, the task of placing those ethics in a hierarchy cannot be set aside. In a conversation with Greg Salmieri and Yaron Brook, Peterson said: '[I]t's not that the world is made of objects'; rather, 'the world is made of what objects to your stupid theory'. The atrocities of the twentieth century are the world's forceful objection to utopian theories. Immunizing certain beliefs from refutation by calling them religious will only slow the absorption of that vital lesson.

It would be benign if '[t]he God of Islam, Judaism and Christianity' (Peterson 1999, p. 144) were just a cosmic back-drop defying all description. I can live with deism. However, if we are to believe the believers, God holds very specific views on topics such as masturbation and newspaper cartoons. Because the actions recommended by religious texts purport-edly hold for everyone, religions are a prelude to politics ('blasphemy' is a particularly dangerous notion, because not only does it object to believers showing a lack of reverence for some deity and/or rituals, it also objects to *non-believers* showing a lack of reverence). Interpretations of God's alleged motives are not answerable to any discernible constraint, so one can invoke God to explain whatever creed one likes and explain away whatever creed one dislikes. Deism rarely stays deistic for long.

As we saw in Chapter 7, debates are futile unless we can first specify the difference(s) a given choice of label makes. I take a theist to be someone who stands ready to do something just because God orders it. Does God command you to do good because it is good, or is the good good because God commands it? If it's the former, then morality does not need God. If it's the latter, then any action (murder, rape, etc.) is only one divine edict away from being okay. If fans of Peterson claim to have rid their religious conviction of supernatural and dogmatic elements, then for all intents and purposes they have rid themselves of religious conviction.

Peterson takes pains to argue that a religious emphasis on the individual translates into individualism, but his arguments overlook the possibility that, when it is grounded in religion, an emphasis on the individual paves the way for an individual leader. When there is no discernible way to adjudicate claims to know God's will, the most tenacious mouthpiece wins. This much is captured by Darwinian theory. The events that happened 'in the first three-quarters of the twentieth century' (Peterson 1999, p. 245) thus give an ominous spin to the idea that '[i]n the "City of God"—that is, the archetypal human kingdom—the Messiah eternally rules' (1999, p. 187).

At a Liberty University convocation where Peterson was the guest speaker, one religious panel member, David Nasser, expressed disappointment that Peterson's latest book offers us 'rules without a ruler'. As I see it, selection pressures are slowly hammering into *Homo sapiens* a revolutionary idea: *one can and should live by rules without living under a ruler*—real or projected. Future generations will have no trouble accepting this, since (I surmise that) this idea will eventually seep into common sense.

They will also have no trouble seeing that the inference 'If God does not exist, then everything is permitted' (Lewy 2008) does not follow.

Of course, in keeping with Peterson's insistence that 'description of the domain of morality tends to exceed the capability of declarative thought' (1999, p. 230), individuals will act out their atheism and *de facto* reliance on rational self-interest long before they officially admit it in their narratives. When a ruler is gone and people become free, there is always a long transition period, like 'when the members of totalitarian cultures such as the modern North Korean collapse into genuine hysteria as a consequence of the death of their leader, who is the embodiment of order and determinate meaning' (Peterson 1999, pp. 206–07). But, like the North Koreans, secular humans will survive, improve their myths, and eventually be better off. The story we humans are telling is far from over.

References

Al-Ghazali. 1963. *Incoherence of the Philosophers*. Translated by Sabih Ahmad Kamali. Lahore: Pakistan Philosophical Congress.

Ashford, Bruce. 2020. 'Jordan Peterson and the Chaos of Our Secular Age'. In *Myth and Meaning: A Christian Appraisal of Jordan Peterson*, edited by Ron Dart, pp. 7–29. Bellingham: Lexham Press.

Averroes. 1987. *The Incoherence of the Incoherence, Volumes I and II*. Translated by Simon Van Den Bergh. Cambridge: E.J.W. Gibb Memorial Trust.

Bacon, Francis. 1902. *Novum Organum*. Edited by Joseph Devey. New York: P.F. Collier.

Baden, Joel S. 2012. *The Composition of the Pentateuch: Renewing the Documentary Hypothesis*. New Haven: Yale University Press.

Baker, Hunter. 2020. 'Peterson the Counter-Revolutionary: Marxism, Postmodern Neo-Marxism, and Suffering'. In *Myth and Meaning: A Christian Appraisal of Jordan Peterson*, edited by Ron Dart, pp. 30–47. Bellingham: Lexham Press.

Beauvoir, Simone de. 2004. *Philosophical Writings*. Edited by Margaret A. Simons, Marybeth Timmermann, and Mary Beth Mader. Urbana: University of Illinois Press.

Beckner, Stephen. 2018. 'Thought Crimes: Jordan Peterson and the Meaning of the Meaning of Life'. *Skeptic*, vol. 23, no. 3, pp. 26–34.

Beverley, James A. 2018. *Understanding Jordan Peterson: A Road Map to the World's Most Controversial Academic*. Second edition. Belleville: Burst Impressions.

Blackwood, Stephen. 2019. 'Cambridge University's Shameful Treatment of Jordan Peterson'. *Quillette*, April 3.

Bloom, Benjamin (Ed.). 1956. *Taxonomy of Educational Objectives: The Classification of Educational Goals*. London: Longmans.

Bonhoeffer, Dietrich. 1959. *Prisoner for God: Letters and Papers from Prison*. Translated by Reginald H. Fuller. New York: Macmillan.

Brierley, John Keith. 1987. *Give Me a Child Until He is Seven: Brain Studies and Early Childhood Education*. London: Taylor and Francis.

Britting, Jeffrey. 2004. *Ayn Rand*. New York: Overlook.

Bruner, Jerome. 2004. 'Life as Narrative'. *Social Research*, vol. 71, no. 3, pp. 691–710.

Bulbulia Joseph, and Uffe Schjoedt. 2010. 'Religious Culture and Cooperative Prediction under Risk: Perspectives from Social Neuroscience'. In *Religion, Economy, and Cooperation*, edited by Ilkka Pyysiäinen, pp. 35–59. Berlin: De Gruyter.

Burke, Thomas Patrick. 2010. 'The Origins of Social Justice: Taparelli d'Azeglio'. *Modern Age*, vol. 52, no. 2, pp. 97–108.

Burston, Daniel. 2019. 'It's Hip to be Square! The Myths of Jordan Peterson'. *Psychotherapy and Politics International*, vol. 17, no. 1, e1475.

Burton, Caitlin M., Jason E. Plaksa, Jordan B. Peterson. 2015. 'Why Do Conservatives Report Being Happier Than Liberals? The Contribution of Neuroticism'. *Journal of Social and Political Psychology*, vol. 3, no. 1, pp. 89–102.

Butler, Andrew C., Jason E. Chapman, Evan M. Forman, and Aaron T. Beck. 2006. 'The Empirical Status of Cognitive-Behavioral Therapy: A Review of Meta-Analyses'. *Clinical Psychology Review*, vol. 26, no. 1, pp. 17–31.

Carver, Charles S., and Scheier, Michael F. 1982. 'Control Theory: A Useful Conceptual Framework for Personality, Social, Clinical, and Health Psychology'. *Psychological Bulletin*, vol. 92, no. 1, pp. 111–135.

Champagne, Marc. 2011a. 'Axiomatizing Umwelt Normativity'. *Sign Systems Studies*, vol. 39, no. 1, pp. 9–59.

Champagne, Marc. 2011b. 'What About Suicide Bombers? A Terse Response to a Terse Objection'. *The Journal of Ayn Rand Studies*, vol. 11, no. 2, pp. 233–236.

Champagne, Marc. 2013. 'Choosing between the Long and Short Informational Routes to Psychological Explanation'. *Philosophical Psychology*, vol. 26, no. 1, pp. 129–138.

Champagne, Marc. 2014. 'Review of Group Agency'. *Philosophy of the Social Sciences*, vol. 44, no. 2, pp. 252–258.

Champagne, Marc. 2015a. 'Disjunctivism and the Ethics of Disbelief'. *Philosophical Papers*, vol. 44, no. 2, pp. 139–163.

Champagne, Marc. 2015b. 'Experience and Life as Ever-Present Constraints on Knowledge'. *Metaphilosophy*, vol. 46, no. 2, pp. 235–245.

Champagne, Marc. 2015c. 'A Less Simplistic Metaphysics: Peirce's Layered Theory of Meaning as a Layered Theory of Being'. *Sign Systems Studies*, vol. 43, no. 4, pp. 523–552.

Champagne, Marc. 2016a. 'Diagrams of the Past: How Timelines can Aid the Growth of Historical Knowledge'. *Cognitive Semiotics*, vol. 9, no. 1, pp. 11–44.

Champagne, Marc. 2016b. 'God, Human Memory, and the Certainty of Geometry: An Argument against Descartes'. *Philosophy and Theology*, vol. 28, no. 2, pp. 299–310.

Champagne, Marc. 2016c. 'Peat Bogs, Sperm and Family Values: Teaching Naturalism Charitably'. *Sexuality and Culture*, vol. 20, no. 3, pp. 526–534.

Champagne, Marc. 2016d. 'Tracking Inferences is not enough: The Given as Tie-Breaker'. *Logos and Episteme*, vol. 7, no. 2, pp. 129–135.

Champagne, Marc. 2018a. *Consciousness and the Philosophy of Signs*. Cham: Springer.

Champagne, Marc. 2018b. 'Semiotics'. *Oxford Bibliographies in Philosophy*. DOI:10.1093/OBO/9780195396577-0179.

Champagne, Marc. 2020. 'Day Shift God, Night Shift God'. *Think*, vol. 19, no. 54, pp. 81–88.

Champagne, Marc, and Mimi Reisel Gladstein. 2015. 'Beauvoir and Rand: Asphyxiating People, Having Sex, and Pursuing a Career'. *The Journal of Ayn Rand Studies*, vol. 15, no. 1, pp. 23–41.

Cimino, Richard, and Christopher Smith. 2007. 'Secular Humanism and Atheism beyond Progressive Secularism'. *Sociology of Religion*, vol. 68, no. 4, pp. 407–424.

Clark, Andy. 2013. 'Whatever Next? Predictive Brains, Situated Agents, and the Future of Cognitive Science'. *Behavioral and Brain Sciences*, vol. 36, no. 3, pp. 181–204.

Cofnas, Nathan, Neema Parvini, Rosalind Arden, Neven Sesardic, and Jonathan Anomaly. 2018. 'The Grievance Studies Scandal: Five Academics Respond'. *Quillette*, October 1.

Cosmides, Leda, and John Tooby. 1992. 'Cognitive Adaptations for Social Exchange'. In *The Adapted Mind: Evolutionary Psychology and the Generation of Culture*, edited by Jerome H. Barkow, Leda Cosmides, and John Tooby, pp. 163–228. New York: Oxford University Press.

Crick, Francis. 1968. 'The Origin of the Genetic Code'. *Journal of Molecular Biology*, vol. 38, no. 3, pp. 367–379.

Csekő, Imre. 2018. 'Az értelmes életcél tartja meg az embert katasztrófa idején'. *Magyar Nemzet*, July 1.

Dart, Ron. 2020. 'Myth, Memoricide, and Jordan Peterson'. In *Myth and Meaning: A Christian Appraisal of Jordan Peterson*, edited by Ron Dart, pp. 67–81. Bellingham: Lexham Press.

Dawkins, Richard. 2006a. *The God Delusion*. London: Bantam Press.

Dawkins, Richard. 2006b. *The Selfish Gene*. 30th anniversary edition. Oxford: Oxford University Press.

Day, Vox. 2018. *Jordanetics: A Journey into the Mind of Humanity's Greatest Thinker*. Kouvola: Castalia House.

Degutis, Algirdas. 2006. 'Deconstructing Postmodern Xenophilia'. *The Journal of Ayn Rand Studies*, vol. 8, no. 1, pp. 49–62.

Degutis, Algirdas. 2007. 'Reflections on Western Self-Deconstruction: Extinction via Liberal Openness'. *Athena*, vol. 3, pp. 31–51.

DeLuca, Kevin Michael. 2007. 'A Wilderness Environmentalism Manifesto: Contesting the Infinite Self-absorption of Humans'. In *Environmental Justice and Environmentalism: The Social Justice Challenge to the Environmental Movement*, edited by Ronald Sandler and Phaedra C. Pezzullo, pp. 27–55. Cambridge: MIT Press.

Delle Fave, Antonella, Fausto Massimini, and Marta Bassi. 2010. *Psychological Selection and Optimal Experience Across Cultures: Social Empowerment through Personal Growth*. Dordrecht: Springer.

Dennett, Daniel C. 2006. *Breaking the Spell: Religion as a Natural Phenomenon*. New York: Viking.

Dewey, John. 1958. *Experience and Nature*. Second revised edition. New York: Dover.

Doidge, Norman. 2018. 'Foreword'. In Jordan B. Peterson, *12 Rules for Life: An Antidote to Chaos*, pp. vii–xxiv. Toronto: Random House.

Dover, Alison G. 2015. '"Promoting Acceptance" or "Preparing Warrior Scholars": Variance in Teaching for Social Justice Vision and Praxis'. *Equity and Excellence in Education*, vol. 48, no. 3, pp. 361–372.

Draper, Paul. 2017. 'Atheism and Agnosticism'. *The Stanford Encyclopedia of Philosophy*, edited by Edward N. Zalta.

Dyson, Michael, Michelle Goldberg, Stephen Fry, and Jordan B. Peterson. 2018. *Political Correctness: The Munk Debates*. Edited by Rudyard Griffiths. Toronto: House of Anansi Press.

Eco, Umberto. 1990. *The Limits of Interpretation*. Bloomington: Indiana University Press.

Engel, Pascal. 2005. 'Belief as a Disposition to Act: Variations on a Pragmatist Theme'. *Cognitio*, vol. 6, no. 2, pp. 167–185.

Fein, Esther B. 1991. 'Book Notes: Influential Book'. *The New York Times*, November 20, p. 00026.

Festinger, Leon. 1957. *A Theory of Cognitive Dissonance*. Stanford: Stanford University Press.

Frankl, Viktor E. 2006. *Man's Search for Meaning: An Introduction to Logotherapy*. Translated by Ilse Lasch. Boston: Beacon Press.

Frye, Northrop. 1982. *The Great Code: The Bible and Literature*. New York: Harcourt Brace Jovanovich.

Glouberman, Mark. 2019. *"I AM": Monotheism and the Philosophy of the Bible*. Toronto: University of Toronto Press.

Goldschmidt, Richard. 1940. *The Material Basis of Evolution*. New Haven: Yale University Press.

Gottschall, Jonathan. 2013. *The Storytelling Animal: How Stories Make Us Human*. Boston: Mariner.

Gould, Stephen Jay, and Elisabeth S. Vrba. 1982. 'Exaptation—A Missing Term in the Science of Form'. *Paleobiology*, vol. 8, no. 1, pp. 4–15.

Gray, John. 2018. *The Seven Types of Atheism*. New York: Farrar, Straus and Giroux.

Haidt, Jonathan. 2012. *The Righteous Mind: Why Good People are Divided by Politics and Religion*. New York: Vintage.

Handa, Sahil. 2019. 'What Conservatives Get Wrong about the Campus Wars'. *National Review*, July 4.

Harriman, David (Ed.). 1999. *Journals of Ayn Rand*. New York: Plume.

Harris, Sam. 2004. *The End of Faith: Religion, Terror, and the Future of Reason*. New York: W.W. Norton.

Harris, Sam. 2007. 'Religion as a Black Market for Irrationality'. *Washington Post/Newsweek*, September 27.

Harris, Sam. 2008. *Letter to a Christian Nation*. New York: Vintage.

Harris, Sam. 2010. *The Moral Landscape: How Science Can Determine Human Values*. New York: Free Press.

Heidegger, Martin. 1996. *Being and Time: A Translation of* Sein und Zeit. Translated by Joan Stambaugh. Albany: State University of New York Press.

Heying, Heather E. 2017. 'First, They Came for the Biologists'. *Wall Street Journal*, October 2.

Hicks, Stephen R.C. 2004. *Explaining Postmodernism: Skepticism and Socialism from Rousseau to Foucault*. Tempe: Scholargy.

Hicks, Stephen R.C., and David C. Kelley. 1998. *Readings for Logical Analysis*. Second edition. New York: W.W. Norton.

Higgins, Heather R. 2018. 'How Philosopher Jordan Peterson Will Change the World'. *The Hill*, May 30.

Hirata, Satoshi, Kunio Watanabe, and Masao Kawai. 2008. '"Sweet-Potato Washing" Revisited'. In *Primate Origins of Human Cognition and Behavior*, edited by Tetsuro Matsuzawa, pp. 487–508. Tokyo: Springer.

Hirsh, Jacob B., Colin G. DeYoung, Xiaowen Xu, and Jordan B. Peterson. 2010. 'Compassionate Liberals and Polite Conservatives: Associations of Agreeableness with Political Ideology and Moral Values'. *Personality and Social Psychology Bulletin*, vol. 36, no. 5, pp. 655–664.

Hirsh, Jacob B., Megan D. Walberg, and Jordan B. Peterson. 2013. 'Spiritual Liberals and Religious Conservatives'. *Social Psychological and Personality Science*, vol. 4, no. 1, pp. 14–20.

Hitchens, Christopher. 2007. *God is Not Great: How Religion Poisons Everything*. Toronto: McClelland and Stewart.

Hopper, Tristin. 2017. 'Here's the Full Recording of Wilfrid Laurier Reprimanding Lindsay Shepherd for Showing a Jordan Peterson Video'. *National Post*, November 20.

Hume, David. 1960. *A Treatise of Human Nature*. Edited by Lewis A. Selby-Bigge. Oxford: Clarendon Press.

Isbell, Lynne A. 2009. *The Fruit, the Tree, and the Serpent: Why We See So Well*. Cambridge: Harvard University Press.

James, William. 2007. *The Principles of Psychology*. Vol. 1. New York: Cosimo.

James, William. 1916. *Talk to Teachers on Psychology*. New York: Henry Holt.

James, William. 1977. *The Writings of William James: A Comprehensive Edition*. Edited by John J. McDermott. Chicago: University of Chicago Press.

Jenkins, Richard. 2000. 'Disenchantment, Enchantment and Re-Enchantment: Max Weber at the Millennium'. *Max Weber Studies*, vol. 1, no. 1, pp. 11–32.

Johnson, Matt. 2018. 'The Peculiar Opacity of Jordan Peterson's Religious Views'. *Quillette*, July 23.

Jost, John T., Chistopher M. Federico, Jaime L. Napier. 2009. 'Political Ideology: Its Structure, Functions, and Elective Affinities'. *Annual Review of Psychology*, vol. 60, pp. 307–337.

Jung, Carl G. 1960. 'Good and Evil in Analytical Psychology'. *Journal of Analytical Psychology*, vol. 5, no. 2, pp. 91–100.

Jung, Carl G. 1968. *The Collected Works of C.G. Jung, Vol. 12: Psychology and Alchemy*. Translated by Richard F.C. Hull. Princeton: Princeton University Press.

Jung, Carl G. 2014. *Archetypes of the Collective Unconscious*. Translated by Gerhard Adler and Richard F.C. Hull. Princeton: Princeton University Press.

Kant, Immanuel. 1993. *Grounding for the Metaphysics of Morals*. Translated by James W. Ellington. Indianapolis: Hackett.

Kearney, Richard. 2011. *Anatheism: Returning to God After God*. New York: Columbia University Press.

Kelley, David C. 2014. *The Art of Reasoning*. Fourth edition. New York: W.W. Norton.

Keltner, Dacher, and Jonathan Haidt. 2003. 'Approaching Awe, a Moral, Spiritual, and Aesthetic Emotion'. *Cognition and Emotion*, vol. 17, no. 2, pp. 297–314.

Khawaja, Irfan. 2014. 'Randian Egoism: Time to Get High'. *Reason Papers*, vol. 36, no. 1, pp. 211–223.

Klein, Daniel B. 2018. 'On Jordan Peterson, Postmodernism, and PoMo-Bashing'. *Society*, vol. 55, no. 6, pp. 477–481.

Kohlberg, Lawrence. 1969. 'Stage and Sequence: The Cognitive-Developmental Approach to Socialization'. In *Handbook of Socialization Theory and Research*, edited by David A. Goslin, pp. 347–480. Chicago: Rand McNally.

Kotter, David S. 2012. *Check Your Premises: Ayn Rand Through a Biblical Lens*. McLean: Institute for Faith, Work and Economics.

Kuhn, Thomas S. 1996. *The Structure of Scientific Revolutions*. Chicago: University of Chicago Press.

Lavrin, Janko. 1969. 'A Note on Nietzsche and Dostoevsky'. *Russian Review*, vol. 28, no. 2, pp. 160–170.

Law, Stephen. 2018. 'Miss the Target: How Some "Sophisticated" Theists Dodge Atheist Criticism'. *Think*, vol. 17, no. 50, pp. 5–13.

Lawrence, Paul R., and Nitin Nohria. 2002. *Driven: How Human Nature Shapes Our Choices*. San Francisco: Jossey-Bass.

Legg, Catherine. 2014. 'Charles Peirce's Limit Concept of Truth'. *Philosophy Compass*, vol. 9, no. 3, pp. 204–213.

Levinas, Emmanuel. 2008. *Totality and Infinity: An Essay on Exteriority*. Translated by Alphonso Lingis. Pittsburgh: Duquesne University Press.

Lewy, Guenter. 2008. *If God is Dead, Everything is Permitted?* New York: Routledge.

Lott, Tim. 2018. 'Jordan Peterson: "The Pursuit of Happiness is a Pointless Goal"'. *The Guardian*, January 21.

Lovins, Tylor S. 2018. *Why Tell the Truth: An Introduction to the Basic Ideas of Jordan B. Peterson*. With a foreword by Alastair J. Roberts. Independently published.

Lukianoff, Greg, and Jonathan Haidt. 2018. *The Coddling of the American Mind: How Good Intentions and Bad Ideas Are Setting up a Generation for Failure*. New York: Penguin.

Lyotard, Jean-François. 1979. *La condition postmoderne : rapport sur le savoir*. Paris: Minuit.

Machan, Tibor R. 2007. '*Atlas Shrugged*'s Moral Principle of the Sanction of the Victim'. In *Ayn Rand's* Atlas Shrugged*: A Philosophical and Literary Companion*, edited by Edward W. Younkins, pp. 75–88. Aldershot: Ashgate.

Mackie, John L. 1977. *Ethics: Inventing Right and Wrong*. New York: Penguin.

Mar, Raymond A. 2004. 'The Neuropsychology of Narrative: Story Comprehension, Story Production and their Interrelation'. *Neuropsychologia*, vol. 42, no. 10, pp. 1414–1434.

Markey-Towler, Brendan. 2018. 'Antifragility, the Black Swan and Psychology: A Psychological Theory of Adaptability in Evolutionary Economies'. *Evolutionary and Institutional Economics Review*, vol. 15, no. 2, pp. 367–384.

Marsh, Leslie. 2018. 'Pathologizing Ideology, Epistemic Modesty and Instrumental Rationality'. In *The Mystery of Rationality: Mind, Beliefs and the Social Sciences*, edited by Gérald Bronner and Francesco Di Iorio, pp. 165–190. Cham: Springer.

Massanari, Adrienne L., and Shira Chess. 2018. 'Attack of the 50-Foot Social Justice Warrior: The Discursive Construction of SJW Memes as the Monstrous Feminine'. *Feminist Media Studies*, vol. 18, no. 4, pp. 525–542.

Merrill, Ronald E. 1991. *The Ideas of Ayn Rand*. Chicago: Open Court.

McDowell, John H. 2002. *Mind and World*. Second edition. Cambridge: Harvard University Press.

Mill, John Stuart. 2002. *On Liberty*. Mineola: Dover.

Morisano, Dominique, Jacob B. Hirsh, Jordan B. Peterson, Robert O. Pihl, and Bruce M. Shore. 2010. 'Setting, Elaborating, and Reflecting on Personal Goals Improves Academic Performance'. *Journal of Applied Psychology*, vol. 95, no. 2, pp. 255–264.

Muldoon, Ryan. 2017. 'Free Speech and Learning from Difference'. *Society*, vol. 54, no. 4, pp. 331–336.

Murphy, Rex. 2019. 'The Yaniv Outrage has Left Canada, Rightly, the Laughing Stock of the World'. *National Post*, July 27.

Murray, Douglas. 2019. 'Antifa's Attack on the Truth'. *UnHerd*, July 5.

Nietzsche, Friedrich. 1966. *Beyond Good and Evil: Prelude to a Philosophy of the Future*. Translated by Walter Kaufmann. New York: Vintage.

Nietzsche, Friedrich. 2005. *The Anti-Christ, Ecce Homo, Twilight of the Idols and Other Writings*. Edited by Aaron Ridley and Judith Norman. Cambridge: Cambridge University Press.

O'Hara, Kieron. 2019. 'Conservatism Then and Now'. *Cosmos + Taxis*, vol. 6, nos. 3–4, pp. 45–51.

Ohlheiser, Abby. 2015. 'Why "Social Justice Warrior", a Gamergate Insult, is now a Dictionary Entry'. *The Washington Post*, October 7.

Peirce, Charles Sanders. 1931–58. *The Collected Papers of Charles Sanders Peirce*. 8 vols. Edited by Charles Hartshorne, Paul Weiss, and Arthur W. Burks. Cambridge: Harvard University Press.

Penk, Alex. 2019. 'Jordan Peterson, and Why We Need to Have "Anti-Fragile" Conversations'. *Stuff*, February 20.

Peterson, Jordan B., Jennifer Rothfleisch, Philip D. Zelazo, and Robert O. Pihl. 1990. 'Acute Alcohol Intoxication and Cognitive Functioning'. *Journal of Studies on Alcohol*, vol. 51, no. 2, pp. 114–122.

Peterson, Jordan B. 1999. *Maps of Meaning: The Architecture of Belief*. New York: Routledge.

Peterson, Jordan B. 2004. 'The Meaning of Meaning'. *International Journal of Existential Psychology and Psychotherapy*, vol. 1, no. 2, pp. 1–13.

Peterson, Jordan B. 2018a. *12 Rules for Life: An Antidote to Chaos*. Toronto: Random House.

Peterson, Jordan B. 2018b. 'Foreword'. In Aleksandr Solzhenitsyn, *The Gulag Archipelago*, pp. xii–xxiii. New York: Penguin Random House.

Peterson, Jordan B. 2019a. 'Gender Politics has No Place in the Classroom'. *National Post*, June 21.

Peterson, Jordan B. 2019b. 'I Wish Cambridge's Faculty of Divinity the Obscurity it Deeply Deserves'. *National Post*, March 21.

Peterson, Jordan B., and Joseph L. Flanders. 2002. 'Complexity Management Theory: Motivation for Ideological Rigidity and Social Conflict'. *Cortex*, vol. 38, no. 4, pp. 429–458.

Piaget, Jean. 1970. *Genetic Epistemology*. Translated by Eleanor Duckworth. New York: W.W. Norton.

Piaget, Jean. 2013. *The Moral Judgment of the Child*. Translated by Marjorie Gabain. London: Routledge.

Popper, Karl. 1971. *The Open Society and its Enemies*. 2 vols. Princeton: Princeton University Press.

Popper, Karl. 1979. *Objective Knowledge: An Evolutionary Approach*. Oxford: Clarendon Press.

Popper, Karl. 2002. *Conjectures and Refutations: The Growth of Scientific Knowledge*. London: Routledge and Kegan Paul.

Proser, Jim. 2020. *Savage Messiah: How Jordan Peterson is Saving Western Civilization*. New York: St. Martin's Press.

Putnam, Hilary. 2002. *The Collapse of the Fact/Value Dichotomy and Other Essays*. Cambridge: Harvard University Press.

Putnam, Hilary, and Ruth Anna Putnam. 2017. *Pragmatism as a Way of Life: The Lasting Legacy of William James and John Dewey*. Edited by David MacArthur. Cambridge: Harvard University Press.

Quine, Willard Van Orman. 1961. *From a Logical Point of View: Nine Logico-Philosophical Essays*. Second edition. New York: Harper Torchbooks.

Rand, Ayn. 1957. *Atlas Shrugged*. New York: Signet.

Rand, Ayn. 1999. *Return of the Primitive: The Anti-Industrial Revolution*. New York: Meridian.

Rasmussen, Douglas B., and Douglas J. Den Uyl. 2005. *Norms of Liberty: A Perfectionist Basis for Non-Perfectionist Politics*. University Park: Pennsylvania State University Press.

Ridgway, Shannon. 2012. 'Oppression Olympics: The Games We Shouldn't Be Playing'. *Everyday Feminism*, November 4.

Roberts, Alastair. 2020. 'Language and Freedom: Peterson as Champion of Free Speech (and Freedom from Compelled Speech)'. In *Myth and Meaning: A Christian Appraisal of Jordan Peterson*, edited by Ron Dart, pp. 48–66. Bellingham: Lexham Press.

Robinson, Nathan J. 2018. 'The Intellectual We Deserve'. *Current Affairs*, March 14.

Rogers, Carl R. 1965. *Client-Centered Therapy: Its Current Practice, Implications, and Theory*. Boston: Houghton Mifflin.

Rogers, Carl R., and Richard E. Farson. 1957. *Active Listening*. Chicago: University of Chicago Industrial Relations Center.

Rorty, Richard. 1979. *Philosophy and the Mirror of Nature*. Princeton: Princeton University Press.

Rosch, Eleanor. 1978. 'Principles of Categorization'. In *Cognition and Categorization*, edited by Eleanor Rosch and Barbara B. Lloyd, pp. 27–48. Hillsdale: Lawrence Erlbaum.

Sartwell, Crispin. 2014. 'The Left-Right Political Spectrum is Bogus'. *The Atlantic*, June 20.

Schellenberg, John L. 2013. 'My Stance in Philosophy of Religion'. *Religious Studies*, vol. 49, vol. 2, pp. 143–150.

Schippers, Michaéla C., Ad W.A. Scheepers, and Jordan B. Peterson. 2015. 'A Scalable Goal-Setting Intervention Closes Both the Gender and Ethnic Minority Achievement Gap'. *Palgrave Communications*, vol. 1, no. 15014, pp. 1–12.

Sciabarra, Chris M. 2000. *Total Freedom: Toward a Dialectical Libertarianism*. University Park: Pennsylvania State University Press.

Scruton, Roger. 2009. *The Roger Scruton Reader*. Edited by Mark Dooley. London: Continuum.

Segal, Robert A. 1999. *Theorizing about Myths*. Amherst: University of Massachusetts Press.

Shapiro, Ben. 2013. *Bullies: How the Left's Culture of Fear and Intimidation Silences Americans*. New York: Threshold.

Shermer, Michael. 2018. 'Have Archetype—Will Travel: The Jordan Peterson Phenomenon'. *Skeptic*, vol. 23, no. 3, pp. 19-24.

Shweder, Richard A., Nancy C. Much, Manamohan Mahapatra, and Lawrence Park. 1997. 'The "Big Three" of Morality (Autonomy, Community, Divinity) and the "Big Three" Explanations of Suffering'. In *Morality and Health*, edited by Allan M. Brandt and Paul Rozin, pp. 119-169. New York: Routledge.

Siamdoust, Nahid. 2018. 'Why Iranian Women Are Taking Off Their Head Scarves'. *The New York Times*, February 5, p. A21.

Smart, J.J.C., and Bernard Williams. 1973. *Utilitarianism: For and Against*. Cambridge: Cambridge University Press.

Smith, Huston. 2001. *Why Religion Matters: The Fate of the Human Spirit in an Age of Disbelief*. New York: Harper Collins.

Smith, Tara. 1998. 'Rights, Wrongs, and Aristotelian Egoism: Illuminating the Rights/Care Dichotomy'. *Journal of Social Philosophy*, vol. 29, no. 2, pp. 5-14.

Smith, Tara. 2006. *Ayn Rand's Normative Ethics: The Virtuous Egoist*. Cambridge: Cambridge University Press.

Solzhenitsyn, Aleksandr I. 2018. *The Gulag Archipelago*. With a foreword by Jordan B. Peterson. New York: Penguin Random House.

Stamos, David N. 2008. *Evolution and the Big Questions: Sex, Race, Religion, and other Matters*. Malden: Blackwell.

Stacey, Timothy. 2018. *Myth and Solidarity in the Modern World: Beyond Religious and Political Division*. Abingdon: Routledge.

Stea, Jonathan N. 2018. 'Jordan Peterson's Endeavor'. *Skeptic*, vol. 23, no. 3, p. 25.

Stein, Murray. 1998. *Jung's Map of the Soul: An Introduction*. Chicago: Open Court.

Steem, Matthew, and Joy Steem. 2020. 'Being and Meaning: Jordan Peterson's Antidote to Evil'. In *Myth and Meaning: A Christian Appraisal of Jordan Peterson*, edited by Ron Dart, pp. 184–201. Bellingham: Lexham Press.

Taleb, Nassim Nicholas. 2007. *The Black Swan: The Impact of the Highly Improbable*. New York: Random House.

Taleb, Nassim Nicholas. 2014. *Antifragile: Things that Gain from Disorder*. New York: Random House.

Taleb, Nassim Nicholas. 2018. *Skin in the Game: Hidden Asymmetries in Daily Life*. London: Penguin.

Tillich, Paul. 1957. *Dynamics of Faith*. New York: Harper and Row.

Tritt, Shona M., Michael Inzlicht, and Jordan B. Peterson. 2013. 'Preliminary Support for a Generalized Arousal Model of Political Conservatism'. *PLOS One*, vol. 8, no. 12, pp. e83333.

Uexküll, Jakob von. 1982. 'The Theory of Meaning'. *Semiotica*, vol. 42, no. 1, pp. 25–82.

Walters, Sally. 1994. 'Algorithms and Archetypes: Evolutionary Psychology and Carl Jung's Theory of the Collective Unconscious'. *Journal of Social and Evolutionary Systems*, vol. 17, no. 3, pp. 287–306.

Warnock, Geoffrey J. 1958. *English Philosophy since 1900*. Oxford: Oxford University Press.

Weiss, Bari. 2018. 'Meet the Renegades of the Intellectual Dark Web'. *The New York Times*, May 8.

Wernham, James C.S. 1986. 'Alexander Bain on Belief'. *Philosophy*, vol. 61, no. 236, pp. 262–266.

Wilson, Edward O. 1999. *Consilience: The Unity of Knowledge*. New York: Vintage.

Wittgenstein, Ludwig. 2001. *Philosophical Investigations*. Translated by G.E.M. Anscombe. Oxford: Blackwell.

Wong, Paul T.P. 2011. 'Positive Psychology 2.0: Towards a Balanced Interactive Model of the Good Life'. *Canadian Psychology*, vol. 52, no. 2, pp. 69–81.

Xu, Xiaowen, Raymond A. Mar, and Jordan B. Peterson. 2013. 'Does Cultural Exposure Partially Explain the Association Between

Personality and Political Orientation?' *Personality and Social Psychology Bulletin*, vol. 39, no. 11, pp. 1497–1517.

Xu, Xiaowen, and Jordan B. Peterson. 2017. 'Differences in Media Preference Mediate the Link Between Personality and Political Orientation'. *Political Psychology*, vol. 38, no. 1, pp. 55–72.

Younkins, Edward W. 2014. 'Philosophical and Literary Integration in Ayn Rand's *Atlas Shrugged*'. *The Journal of Ayn Rand Studies*, vol. 14, no. 2, pp. 124–147.